WHEN HOMOSEXUALITY INVADES THE FAMILY

(Biblical guidelines for parents, counselors, and daughters)

by

Ruth Ann Bruce

xulon PRESS

Copyright © 2003 by Ruth Ann Bruce

When Homosexuality Invades the Family
by Ruth Ann Bruce

Printed in the United States of America

ISBN 1-594671-86-9

All rights reserved. No part of this publication may be reproduced or transmitted in any form or by any means without written permission of the author.

Unless otherwise indicated, Bible quotations are taken from the New International Version of the Bible. © 1973, 1978,1984 by International Bible Society, Zondervan Publishing House.

Verses marked NASB are taken from the New American Standard Bible © 1960, 1963, 1968, 1971, 1972, 1973, 1975, 1977, by The Lockman Foundation.

Verses marked NKJV are taken from The Holy Bible, New King James Version © 1982 by Thomas Nelson, Inc. New Geneva Study Bible © 1995 by Foundation for Reformation.

Xulon Press
www.XulonPress.com

Xulon Press books are available in bookstores everywhere, and on the Web at www.XulonPress.com.

ENDORCEMENT

◈

WHEN HOMOSEXUALITY INVADES THE FAMILY offers solid biblical help to parents facing one of the most difficult challenges that parents, committed to a biblical perspective on life, may face. The contents are very biblical and practical in terms of expositing relevant Scriptural truth and providing guidelines for what to do if or when what the title suggests occurs. It will certainly be useful for parents who are actually going through this experience, for others who want to understand homosexuality biblically and especially for counselors who are called on to help struggling parents and give instruction to people in general. With compassion and biblical accuracy, Ruth Ann Bruce has written a book that addresses a problem that is becoming increasingly common, but nonetheless extremely painful.

Dr. Wayne Mack

ACKNOWLEDGMENTS

The journey to this book began with a lady who had a vision for Biblical Counseling in Southwest Florida. She was my mentor. Thank you, Rae Burrows, for your deep love for the Scriptures and your belief in its total sufficiency to meet all our needs. You taught me how to care for people and how to counsel them by using God's Word.

Much thanks, also, to The Master's College professors who further helped equip me for counseling — Dr. Stuart Scott, Dr. John Street, Dr. David Smith and Dr. Wayne Mack, my thesis advisor, whose words of encouragement led to my thesis becoming a book.

Thanks to my proofreaders — Kim, Regina, Jackie and Ken, and my computer assistants Lori, Sonya, Vinny and my nephew, Mark. Thanks also to those who gave me much encouragement — my sister, Loretta, Jackie, Ginny, Shirley, Lynn, Valerie, Lori, Irene, and the ladies in my Bible study groups.

I especially want to thank my family. "Go for it, Mom!" was my daughters' response, after being informed that their mom was going back for her master's degree. This would not have been possible without the help and support of my sweetheart and husband of 43 years. He is truly a blessing from God.

CONTENTS

I. INTRODUCTION 9
II. DEALING WITH THE HEARTBREAK 15
III. FAMILY STRUGGLES HANDLED BIBLICALLY 21
IV. THE BIBLICAL VIEW OF HOMOSEXUALITY 25
V. UNBIBLICAL VIEWS REFUTED 43
VI. SHARING THE BURDEN 53
VII. EFFECTIVE PRAYER IN DIFFICULT TIMES 57
VIII. STRAINED RELATIONSHIPS 63
IX. SPIRITUAL GROWTH THROUGH TRIAL 69
X. BIBLICAL COUNSEL FOR DAUGHTERS 81
XI. SUMMARY FOR THE DAUGHTER 103
XII. SUMMARY FOR THE PARENTS 107

VERBATIM COUNSELING — Parents 111

VERBATIM COUNSELING — Daughter 119

APPENDIX 127

ENDNOTES 165

CHAPTER I

INTRODUCTION

∞

One of life's greatest joys is parenthood. With much prayer and under God's guidance, Christian parents strive to rear their children in the fear and admonition of the Lord. Not all children, however, continue to follow the teachings of Scripture as they mature. Instead, they choose what is contrary to it.

Few things are more devastating than to discover that your daughter has chosen to live in homosexuality. This shocking revelation brings anxiety, a sense of hopelessness, and disinterest in life. It saps strength from the body and joy from the soul. It may also bring physical symptoms including nausea, migraines, and sleeplessness. Tears, which often bring relief, are absent. When the shock lessens, though it never really goes away, disbelief sets in, and you begin to doubt the obvious. Thoughts, e.g., "This is not true; a mistake has been made," or "This must be a dream. I will wake up from this nightmare," occupy your mind day and night. The truth, however, is that what you have learned is true. The daughter, whom you raised to love the Lord, who went to church with you regularly and who may even profess to follow the Lord, has turned her back on clear

Biblical teaching to pursue a life of sin.

Parents' responses will vary as they deal with not only the shock and disbelief, but also with a sense of devastation. Some will respond with statements; e.g., "This cannot be happening to our family," or "I cannot take this. This is more than I can handle." Some will respond with questions, e.g., "What do we do now?" or "How will I ever face people?" or "Where can I turn for help? Is there any help?" or "How could this have happened?" Still others will respond in anger. Their response is more rash. They will think and plan to disown their daughter or write her out of their will. They will think of ways to shock her into changing. They will wonder how she could do what she has done and expect things to stay the same.

Christian parents want to understand. How could this have happened? Who is to blame? How could it have been prevented? What is the next step? Biblically dealing with this family crisis requires searching the Scriptures for God's answers and applying the principles. God's Word is relevant and sufficient. Ecclesiastes 1:9b says " . . . there is nothing new under the sun."[1] This verse reminds all believers that no matter how difficult the situation, it is not something brand new. The Bible speaks to the problems of life and has many examples citing those who faced very difficult circumstances, sought God in those circumstances, and lived to tell of His grace.

Stability can come only as you seek God's Word and follow its directions. The account of the prodigal son in Luke 15 tells the story of two sons raised in the same household. The older son was content to remain with his father, serve him diligently, and follow his commands. Year after year, this older son faithfully worked on his father's estate and under his father's tutelage. The younger son, however, decided to strike out on his own and be independent of his father's restraints. He wanted his part of the inheritance early so he could run his own life and make his own decisions apart from his father's guidance.

Both sons were reared basically the same. One chose to be obedient; the other chose to be disobedient. We are not told what, if anything, the father did or said to encourage his son to stay at home. It is clear, however, that the younger son decided he wanted a different lifestyle than the one his father had provided, and he pursued it.

Parents, wiser because of experience and often with far more knowledge than their children, find themselves powerless to do anything to stop a determined child from pursuing a life of sin. Prayer and faith in God, however, are powerful weapons against the evil one's tactics. In Luke's account, we read that the young man came to his senses and made the decision to go home. We are not told how long he had been away from his family in rebellion. What is apparent is that the father had not given up on his son, had not written him off, and had not forgotten him. When the son was a great way off, his father saw him and recognized him as his son. His father had been watching for him, perhaps daily, and was filled with compassion for him. He ran to meet his son, threw his arms around him, and kissed him. The father said, "For this son of mine was dead and is alive again; he was lost and is found" (Luke 15:24).

Stability comes when Christian parents believe and act upon directions and hope from God's Word. First Corinthians 10:13 says that temptations or trials are common to man but God's faithfulness to His children will enable them to bear up under them. God has promised not to put more on His children than they can handle. There is no Biblical reason to believe that God is not going to hold you up and give you the grace to come through this trial, no matter how difficult. God's grace enables believers to stand up under anything He permits to come their way.

Stability does not come easily or quickly. It does not come when people say that everything will be all right, give it time, or things will work out. It does not come when parents choose to separate from their daughter because her very appearance and/or her actions remind them of her sin. Stability comes through active obedience to God's Word and trust in the God of that word. There is a purpose for everything that God brings into our lives. Job's answer to his wife who thought he should curse God and die was, "Shall we accept good from God, and not trouble?" (Job 2:10b). Even before Job's pain was gone, his reply to God was, "I know that you can do all things; no plan of yours can be thwarted" (Job 42:2).

The world uses the argument that a person is born a homosexual, that homosexuality is in the genes. Others say that it is impossible to change one's sexual orientation once they have been imprinted. What we know to be true, however, and according to the teachings of the Bible, is that homosexuality is a sin, and sin has a cure. If homosexuality were a disease or mental disorder, there would be little or no hope. The hope of the child of God is in the fact that the Bible says the blood of Christ cleanses us from all sin.

Parents are neither hopeless nor helpless. Hebrews 4:15 tells us that Jesus, our high priest, sympathizes with us in our weaknesses, and though tempted even as we are, was without sin. And most comforting of all, according to Romans 8:34, is that Christ Jesus is at the right hand of God the Father interceding on our behalf. In addition, verses 26, 27 of the same chapter say the Spirit, Himself, intercedes for us according to the Father's will. The Holy Trinity is working on behalf of those who are following Christ. He knows their heartaches and He cares.

You do not have to live with little or no hope. You do not have to live in devastation. The One who died for you will stay by your side, for He promises never to leave you nor forsake you. He is your confidence; He is your Helper (Heb 13:5, 6).

CHAPTER II

DEALING WITH THE HEARTBREAK

※

God's Word offers comfort to those whose hearts are breaking. Psalm 34:18,19 tell us that the Lord is close to the brokenhearted, and He will save those who are crushed in spirit. The righteous will have trouble, but the Lord has promised to protect and deliver. Psalm 147:3 says the Lord heals the brokenhearted and binds up their wounds.

Parents are incapable of carrying this heartbreak alone. They will need to learn how to cast this heavy burden on the Lord. First Peter 5:7 instructs all believers to "Cast your anxiety on Him because He cares for you." Casting cares on the Lord takes a deliberate act of the will. When thoughts turn to worry, God will help parents change that worry into prayer. When the mind chooses to dwell on hopelessness and fear, a deliberate act will change the focus to verses of Scripture filled with hope. Second Peter 1:3 says, "His divine power has given us everything we need for life and godliness through our knowledge of Him who called us by His own glory and goodness."

Heartache can easily produce loneliness. Parents begin

thinking the Lord has forgotten and forsaken them. The question, "Why?" often comes to mind. David, the man after God's own heart, expressed such a time in his life in Psalm 13. He wanted to know if the Lord had forgotten him—forever. He wanted to know how long he would have to wrestle with his thoughts and have sorrow in his heart. He pled for God to answer him. In verse three, David begins to seek God's face for answers, and in verse five, he makes a deliberate statement, "But I trust in your unfailing love." In the last verse of this Psalm, David is singing to the Lord. He moved from despair to singing.

Parents of homosexual daughters can come through their despair to singing as well. Though they may think sorrow has come to stay and perhaps God has hidden His face from them, they are wrong. Christ said in John 10 that He came that we might have life and have it abundantly. It is not God's will that His children just exist, enduring heartache until He calls them to heaven. Therefore, dealing with the immediate heartache is about casting cares on the Caregiver. It is about trusting in Him who is trustworthy, relying wholeheartedly on Him to help discipline the mind.

The heartbreak that parents experience in the beginning reoccurs as time goes on and no changes are made. First and foremost, their hearts are broken because the daughter is sinning against the Lord. She has chosen to ignore what the Bible says about homosexuality and they fear for her eternal soul. They see her seeking ways to ignore or change Biblical meanings and even adding to or taking from their original intent. Proverbs 30: 5,6 remind them that, "Every word of God is flawless . . . do not add to His words."

Since living in the state of despair is not trusting in the Lord with the heart and all the strength God gives, parents must view the present state of things and any future events with a new focus. Their focus must change from being consumed with their daughter, her choices, and her lifestyle.

It must change from focusing on themselves, their heartache, and all that goes with it. Their focus must change to Christ and His redemptive work and to what God promises in His Word. Parents, who early on want to give up or are afraid they cannot endure, can learn to depend on the Lord and draw strength from Him daily. If this does not happen, they will live a life of defeat, continue to question events of the past, and be ineffective in their walk with Christ.

The Biblical way to overcome heartbreak is to show love to the daughter. This love is not a feeling, nor does it condone the homosexual behavior. Biblical love is based on 1 Corinthians 13 which says, "Love is patient . . . kind. It does not envy, it does not boast. It is not proud . . . self-seeking . . . easily angered . . . It always hopes, always perseveres."

As wonderful as all these verses are, the question persists, "How do parents live and function in a relationship with their daughter in a God-honoring way?" Is preaching to her and quoting verses to her the way to go? Riveted with guilt, parents are willing to try most anything if they think it will work. Month after month goes by, and the daughter appears to be enjoying life to its fullest. The heartache continues because nothing seems to be changing.

Sometimes, there is a ray of hope. Perhaps the daughter's present relationship has broken up and no new one has yet developed. The parents will pray harder and hope more, but unless the daughter has dealt with the issues of the heart, confessed her sin and repented, she will continue in this lifestyle. The hearts of Mom and Dad are once again broken.

Discouraging thoughts, hopes gained and then dashed, create confusion to the already troubled scene. As months roll into years, parents may begin to wonder if they are wrong. Could this lifestyle possibly be acceptable in the eyes of the Lord? The daughter appears to be doing well; she has many friends and is even attending church. What answers do parents give when the daughter insists she loves the Lord and is serving Him? What should be said when she says she is witnessing and leading others to Christ? These are real questions that demand real answers. First John 2:3,4 says, "... we have come to know Him if we obey His commands. The man who says, 'I know Him', but does not do what He commands is a liar, and the truth is not in him." Proverbs 14:12 says, "There is a way that seems right to a man but in the end it leads to death." Paul warns in 1 Corinthians 6:9-11 about being deceived, "... neither the sexually immoral ... nor homosexual offenders ... will inherit the kingdom of God." This is the Word of God. It is clear. It is infallible and it is unchangeable.

The differences in how each side views life become very clear when the parents try to approach the subject of this sinful lifestyle. The wall of resistance quickly rises between the two sides, and it soon becomes apparent that basically nothing has changed. The daughter begins to defend her choices, and the parents answer with words of Scripture. There may even follow a heated discussion, an altercation about Biblical translations and interpretation of Scripture. It all can quickly turn ugly. Ephesians 6:12 becomes very meaningful. It says, "For our struggle is not against flesh and blood, but against the rulers, against the authorities, against the powers of this dark world and against the spiritual forces of evil in the heavenly realms." Confusion and discouragement are part of the spiritual battle for the soul of the daughter.

The Scriptures alone offer the encouragement needed to live each day with the reality that this beloved daughter is living her life in direct opposition to God's Word. This life of sin cannot be acceptable to God. It comes down to this: God's Word versus man's philosophy; glorifying God versus futile thinking and foolish hearts; the truth of God versus Satan's lies; the knowledge of God versus a depraved mind (Rom 1).

The Word of God is what stabilizes the Christian parent in the darkest times of confusion and discouragement. Psalm 19:7,8a declares, "The law of the Lord is perfect, reviving the soul. The statutes of the Lord are trustworthy, making wise the simple. The precepts of the Lord are right, giving joy to the heart." There will be times when the soul will need to be revived—God's law will do that. There will be circumstances and decisions where parents will need great wisdom—God's statues make the simple wise. There will be many seasons of sadness—God's precepts will give joy to the heart.

The interactions and relationship between parents and their daughter will be strained. Many questions will arise regarding something as simple as conversation. It is as though you are talking to a stranger. Our Lord's great example can be very helpful as we study His word. Christ always loves His children, even in their deplorable state, and He continues to reach out to them when they least deserve His love. Parents must do the same.

As difficult as it may be, and regardless of the circumstances, parents are instructed to love. They must love even when their daughter seems more like an enemy. Again, this is not approval in any way of her lifestyle, but it is obedience to Christ's command in John 13:34 where He instructs us to love one another.

With this love, parents must maintain a distinction between 'acceptance' and 'approval'. "'Acceptance' means 'acknowledging what is true'. It recognizes the reality of a person's choices and behavior. 'Approval', on the other hand, means 'affirming something as good or right'."[2] Parents should accept their daughter and love her, but because of the truths of the Bible, they can never approve of her sinful homosexual behavior. After the parents have clearly stated their position regarding what the Word of God says and means, the time has come to back off, love, and pray.

When Jesus wept over Jerusalem, His words, "If you . . . had only known . . .what would bring you peace . . ." tell us the people were going their own way, disregarding the teaching of the law and the prophets. Christ's love was still evident as He wept over them, yearning to help them through life.

The contention between David and Absalom serves as another example of a child's rebellion and sin. David's responses as recorded in 2 Samuel 15-19 are worth consideration. Absalom hated most of what David stood for and determined to do things his own way. Time after time, David's heart was broken; yet his love and concern for Absalom never wavered. Even when it appeared to be Absalom's life or his, David said to deal kindly with his son. His source of strength was the Lord. Psalm 3:5 states, "I lie down and sleep; I wake again, because the Lord sustains me." That is the secret.

When it is hard to sleep, or when sleep serves as an escape, it is the Lord God who will sustain.

See appendix A

CHAPTER III

FAMILY STRUGGLES HANDLED BIBLICALLY

∞

A family that once had harmony and sought to work out problems on a daily basis finds itself in the midst of a struggle. With the preoccupation of a painful reality, tempers are short and responsibilities are left undone. Everyone is consumed with this new revelation. It is as though a death has occurred but with no funeral. What has happened? Surely someone is to blame.

Mom will ask questions similar to the following: Where did I go wrong? What did I do wrong? What did I do that I should not have done? What did I not do correctly? Did I not give enough affection? Too much, perhaps? Did we have meaningful conversations? Were we close enough for her to be comfortable with me? Did we pray together often enough? What might I have done differently? The questions are endless.

The father will ask many of the same questions and also question his leadership role in the home. He will ask: Was I a strong, spiritual leader? How could I have been more effective? Did I pray fervently enough? Perhaps the hardest is, What do I do now? How do I continue to show love without seeming to sanction this sinful behavior? How do we treat her partner or do we keep our distance? The temptation to blame each other must be resisted immediately. As sometimes happens with the death of a child, the marriage relationship, which should become stronger in support for one another, becomes a battleground of blame shifting and accusations. Couples will blame each other for not being strict enough or for being too strict, for not checking out friends more thoroughly, for not guarding activities more closely, and a myriad of other things.

Together, the couple may blame the church and the ineffectiveness of the youth program. They will question how relative the sermons have been over the years to young people and whether the youth has been given enough attention. Maybe the ministry to the youth could have been more poignant and less general. Perhaps the pastor is unaware of the temptations of youth today. Is he out of touch? Does he care enough to make a difference?

Blaming society is another avenue parents travel. Radio and television personalities accept homosexuality as an alternative lifestyle. Sitcoms and talk shows portray it as normal and anyone who opposes it as homophobic. In the book *WHEN THE WICKED TAKE THE CITY*, the author summarizes an article from the homosexual magazine "Guide" written by two homosexual men. To outline strategies designed to weaken the family, "The authors say it's imperative that gays talk about their gayness as much as possible on TV and radio until people become indifferent to homosexuality. Straights will eventually be desensitized to the point that homosexuality will be viewed as just any other lifestyle."[3] The media has bowed to the pressures of the homosexual community, and whether or not they agree with the philosophy, they continue to bombard the airways with its message.

What about the daughter? Should no blame be placed on her? Parents, in anger, will wonder why she did not seek help at the beginning. Perhaps she did seek help but found it of no use since it was sought in the wrong place. Parents will be angry because their daughter was not open and honest in her struggle with sin but chose instead to deceive them over a period of time. Blame might be placed on her because she chose to act on feelings she knew to be in direct opposition to the Bible.

It is foolish, however, to believe a young girl would choose this lifestyle initially. Even though many in society accept this lifestyle as normal for some people, many more frown upon it. It is not an easy way of life because family and friends often become estranged. Young ladies have testified that early in their lives they felt different or out of step with other girls their age. Those from Christian homes say they sought the Lord with tears, asking Him to change their feelings. The following quotes reveal the struggle with homosexuality tendencies at an early age.

"Even at such a young age (elementary school), I recall seeing girls chase boys and vice versa and wanted to be a part of it."

"I used to lie in bed at night and pray that God would send me a boyfriend, thinking that having a boy I liked would make all of the bad feelings go away."

"I hoped that this was just a "stage" and my feelings were just part of a stage of normal development."

Others have testified that because they were sexually abused at a young age, they are now homosexual.

Exodus is an organization that ministers to homosexuals and former homosexuals. "Several Exodus leaders estimate that 80 to 90 percent of the women coming for help to ex-gay ministries have been victimized. In many cases the abuser is a male family member or trusted friend."[4] Abuse can be neither minimized nor ignored, and the proper authorities must be notified. But as high as this figure is, it does not account for all the cases, and perhaps even more important, not every female who was abused chooses the homosexual lifestyle. Not knowing the cause for their daughter's choices, parents will look to blame some event or chain of events or someone in particular. Blame shifting, however, does not benefit anyone, and it certainly does nothing to solve the problem.

Understandably, if a daughter is struggling when she is still living at home and under the direct authority of her parents, she will struggle more when she gets away from home. In a less controlled environment, with fewer restraints and pulls toward ungodliness, involvement in this way of life is sure to be continued and encouraged. Many campuses promote a so-called freedom which includes this "alternative" lifestyle, and for someone already struggling, it can be a difficult thing to resist.

As complicated as the situation may get and having to deal with questions as they continue to pile up, the simple fact remains—the daughter is living a life of sin and needs to repent. Wondering who is to blame or what circumstances contributed to the situation will not solve the problem, mend all differences, or relieve the sorrow in the heart. Although there is nothing wrong with evaluating contributing factors, the daughter has chosen to live her life to please herself above living her life to please the Lord.

CHAPTER IV

THE BIBLICAL VIEW OF HOMOSEXUALITY

∞

OLD TESTAMENT

In the beginning, God designed marriage for a husband and wife; it was God's creation. God gave the husband and his wife a very special relationship and called it "one flesh" (Gen 2:24). He made Adam and Eve in His image, male and female. They were created to bring glory to God as they complemented one another in this relationship. They were instructed to leave all others and cleave to one another. "The Creator's vision of full humanity was of two sexually differentiated components, each of the same stuff, on a-par, the same yet different, finding their fulfillment in mutual surrender . . .within the bounds of mutual male/female commitment, we are called to a frank enjoyment of our sexuality."[5] Yes, God has put boundaries around how sexuality is expressed so that it is not used for purposes other than He intended. There is no relationship as unique as the marriage relationship.

One of the earliest accounts recorded in Genesis is the story of the flood and the reason God deemed it necessary to destroy all but one family. In Genesis 6, we read where God saw how great was the wickedness of men and that the intent of man's heart was evil all the time. Because of the inclination toward wickedness, mankind has perverted some of life's greatest joys. One of the most prevalent perversion is in the area of sexuality. Today, the Christian and the Christian church are pressured to accept behavior that is clearly forbidden by God, and they must be prepared to face these things with clear Biblical answers.

Historical and Biblical studies down through the ages have agreed that the Bible emphatically declares homosexuality to be a sin. The traditional—church view is that homosexuality displeases God and is one of the reasons for Sodom's destruction. This view prevailed until the closing years of the twentieth century. Now, there is an onslaught of redefinitions and reinterpretations so that even some mainline churches are questioning and debating this traditional view. Some are outright denying its validity.

In 1957, as the result of a study concerning homosexuality, the Quakers in England, concluded that homosexuality is natural and morally neutral—neither good nor bad.[6] With a membership around 9 million, the United Methodist Church meeting in San Francisco stated, " . . . an overwhelming majority of those testifying at five public hearings wanted to soften the church's condemnation of gay sex and remove barriers keeping 'self-avowed, practicing homosexuals' from becoming Methodist ministers."[7] In 1991, the Episcopalians began the process for the ordination of non-celibate homosexuals by leaving the decision to the individual diocese. A furor in the Presbyterian Church (USA) concerns the possibility of ordaining practicing homosexuals. One report said that more important than sexual activity, including premarital, marital or postmarital, is responsible relationships. Opponents say this reasoning ignores the Bible.

Second Thessalonians 2 addresses the lawlessness of

man and the deceitfulness which is believed by those who perish. When they refuse to believe the truth, "God sends them a powerful delusion, so that they will believe the lie and so that all will be condemned who have not believed the truth but have delighted in wickedness" (2 Thess 2:11,12). After man refuses the truth for so long, God will cause him to believe a lie.

What *does* the Bible say about homosexuality, and in particular the Old Testament? How are believers to interpret what it says? Genesis 19 gives the famous account of the destruction of the city of Sodom. What is to be learned from this event in history? The Bible gives the account of two angels who arrived in Sodom planning to spend the night in the square. Lot, the only righteous man living there, invited them to spend the night in his home. When they refused, he urged them so strongly that they accepted his invitation. After they had eaten their dinner and before they had retired for the night, the men of the city surrounded the house demanding to have sex with the two men. Their intentions were very clear. "Bring them out to us so that we can have sex with them" (Gen 19:5b). "Bring them out to us that we may have relations with them" (Gen 19:5b NASB). " . . . that we may know them" (Gen 19:5b NKJV). Some individuals who debate the issue of whether the men were seeking a homosexual act have chosen the translation "know them" rather than "have sex with" or "relations with" because they do not want to accept the obvious. They argue that this scene had nothing to do with sexual relations but with getting acquainted with one another.

The term "know" in this context demands that it be interpreted as sexual in meaning. Not only is it clear from the onset, but it is made more clear, if possible, later on when Lot offered his daughters to the men saying that his daughters had never known a man. It would make no sense to interpret this as their "having never gotten acquainted with a man."

Lot appealed to the men of the city, asking them to not act wickedly. "Don't do this wicked thing" (Gen 19:7). When the wicked men were about to break down the door, the angels reached out for Lot, brought him inside, and shut the door. God struck the wicked men with blindness in preparation for Lot's escape. These angels had been sent by God to destroy the wicked city because the outcry to the LORD against it was so great.

The account of the destruction of Sodom shows how wicked the people were, what one of their sins was, and how God dealt with them. The New Testament book of Jude, verse 7, says, "Sodom . . . gave themselves up to sexual immorality and perversion. They serve as an example of those who suffer the punishment of eternal fire." So, not only is the case clear in the Old Testament book of Genesis, its clarity is verified in the New Testament.

Leviticus 18 records the LORD'S words when He spoke to Moses about unlawful sexual relations. "Do not lie with a man as one lies with a woman; that is detestable" (Lev 18:22). "You shall not lie with a male as one lies with a female; it is an abomination" (Lev 18:22 NASB). This command applies to both men and women. Paul makes that very clear in Romans 1:26: "Even their women exchanged natural relations for unnatural ones."

In Leviticus 20:13, homosexuality was considered so detestable that the participants were put to death. Both Leviticus 18:22 and 20:13, along with the exceptional destruction of Sodom for its homosexuality in the patriarchal period, teach the moral prohibition of homosexuality. God condemns homosexuality as unnatural, a severe disorder against creation, and so vile as to warrant death.[8]

In Judges 19, another account is recorded about men wanting to have sex with other men. The men are called wicked, and what they want to do is labeled wickedness. In not one place in all of Scripture is sex between the same sex either regulated or commended. Every mention of homosexuality in God's inspired Word is condemned.

It has been suggested that since the Old Testament does not mention homosexuality between women, the act might not be condemned. Accepting this would mean that lesbianism, which is not a Biblical term, is acceptable behavior solely because the Old Testament does not discuss it. An argument from silence (i.e., if the Bible is silent on a subject it must approve of it) is, of course, a very frail argument. Many types of undesirable sins and sinful relationships could be justified by this line of reasoning.

Among several explanations for the silence about women in the Old Testament is the woman's restrictive life and movement outside the home and the fact that women were expected to bear and raise children. More importantly, moral laws were for everyone—males and females. Again, Romans 1:26 makes that clear. The Biblical principles of the Old Testament are not in opposition to the principles of the New Testament. One testament is not pitted against the other. The moral laws of the Old Testament are reinforced in the New Testament and, at times, are even stronger; e.g., adultery in the Old Testament was the sexual act. In the New Testament, Jesus said that to look at someone lustfully is to commit adultery in the heart.

THE NEW TESTAMENT AND JESUS

Although Jesus did not speak specifically about homosexuality, He did talk about the purposes of God when He created Adam and Eve. In affirmation of the Old Testament, He quoted Genesis 2:24 in answer to the Pharisees concerning divorce (Matt 19:5). The theme for human sexuality, running through the entire Bible from Genesis to Revelation, is always within the bounds and bonds of marriage. It is against this backdrop that sexual behavior should be discussed.

Jesus never departed from the teachings of the Old Testament but in several places, and especially in the Sermon on the Mount, He confirmed its authority. "He considered His own teaching to be an extension and a clarification of the Old Testament not, as is so often supposed, a radical departure from it."[9] In Matthew 5:17, Jesus said He did not come to abolish the law but to fulfill it. In some cases, He raised the standard higher; e.g., anger equals murder and lust equals adultery.

Christ did deal with sexual sin when the woman caught in adultery was brought to Him. His compassion was evident, but He still labeled her act as sin. His compassion for her did not condone what she had done, but He instructed her to "Go now and leave your life of sin" (John 8:11).

Just because homosexuality is not mentioned in the Gospels does not make it acceptable in God's eyes or any less a sin. The Gospels are not above the rest of Scripture; neither are they more important. Furthermore, we cannot be sure that Jesus never spoke about homosexuality. John 16:12 tells us that Jesus had many things to say, but since the people could not bear them at that time, the Holy Spirit, whom He would send, would be the Guide to all truth. It is recorded in John 21:25 that if all the things Jesus did were written down in books, the world itself would not be able to contain them.

Romans 1:26, 27 cannot be understood as anything other than God's displeasure and condemnation regarding any kind of homosexuality. There are those who disagree, and the errors, misinterpretations, and revisions to these verses will be dealt with later in the book.

In Romans 1, beginning with verse 18, Paul begins to speak of the wrath of God toward ungodliness and unrighteousness. He says God's wrath is revealed because men and women choose to suppress the truth in unrighteousness. God has made Himself evident to everyone, since the creation of the world, but men and women have chosen to rebel and reject Him. Truth about God, including His eternal power and divine nature, is plain, so that all are without excuse. Men and women dishonor God, are unthankful, are futile in their thoughts, and are foolish in their hearts. Instead of worshipping the true God, they set up their own gods. The Scriptures calls this idolatry.

Some of the most sobering words from Scripture which God says and repeats twice are "God gave them over" (vv. 24, 26, 28). Why would God give anyone over or up? And, to what would He give them up? In his commentary, Matthew Henry writes, "God gave them up, in a way of righteous judgment, as a just punishment of their idolatry - taking off the bridle of restraining grace - leaving them to themselves - letting them alone."[10] As a result, their carnal hearts were more concerned with pleasing themselves than with pleasing God.

Many daughters have knowledge about God but have, unfortunately, surrendered to the desires and lusts of the heart and are swept into these homosexual encounters. They may have a knowledge of God, but they do not acknowledge God for who He is and what He demands.

Paul continues by informing his readers what this turning from truth produces. They were given over to sexual impurity (v. 24), shameful lusts (v. 26), and a depraved mind (v. 28). "Those who dishonored God were given up to dishonour themselves. A man cannot be delivered up to a greater slavery than to be given up to his own lusts."[11]

One of the expressions of our fallenness is sexual impurity, and one of the sexual impurities is homosexuality. Paul describes how righteousness is exchanged for unrighteousness: the glory of God is exchanged for idols (v. 23); the truth about God is exchanged for a lie (v. 25); women exchanged natural relations with unnatural ones (v. 26); and men exchange natural relations with a woman and are inflamed with lust for one another (v. 27).

When a daughter turns from the proper relationship with her Creator and suppresses the truth of God, various forms of idolatry will begin to manifest themselves. Anything for which she is willing to sin has become her idol. Should she desire to pursue a relationship which God condemns as sin, she has put her desire above God's desire. She must replace the will of God with her own. When her desires are more important to her than God's, and she continues to follow her own desires instead of the clear commands of Scripture, God will give her over to her lusts, and her polluted practice will become a way of life. This is what Paul is talking about in this passage.

Romans 1 is only one of several obvious condemnations of homosexuality in the Bible, and one cannot evade the straightforward charges made here. When Paul draws attention to the women first, saying, "Even their women exchanged natural relations for unnatural ones" (v. 26), Murray says it is "for the purpose of accentuating the grossness of the evil. It is the delicacy which belongs to the woman that makes more apparent the degeneracy of homosexual indulgence in their case."[12] Details, which are missing in regard to women, are spelled out explicitly in verse 27 where male homosexuality is addressed.

So whether the Holy Spirit, through Paul, is speaking of men or women, the fact is that those controlled by homosexual desires and those committing such acts have abandoned what God ordained to be between only a husband and a wife. Both "the creation order and the law of God have been violated in any and all expressions of homosexuality."[13]

John Ankerberg makes five observations about Romans 1. The downward trend toward apostasy and divine judgment proceed in this manner:

1. "Men refuse to accept the intuitive knowledge which

God has placed within them concerning Himself.
2. This results in rebellion against God manifested in idolatry.
3. God begins a process of initial judgment or 'giving over' to sin.
4. This produces, in part, unnatural lusts and perversions.
5. (This) results in a wide variety of additional vices and evils."[14]

The last verse of Romans 1 tells us that those aforementioned knew God's righteous decrees. They knew what was right and what was wrong; yet, they continued to live in their sin and approved of those who did likewise.

First Corinthians 6:9-11 - "Do you not know that the wicked will not inherit the kingdom of God? Do not be deceived: Neither the sexually immoral nor idolaters nor adulterers nor male prostitutes nor homosexual offenders nor thieves nor the greedy nor drunkards nor slanderers nor swindlers will inherit the kingdom of God. And that is what some of you were. But you were washed, you were sanctified, you were justified in the name of the Lord Jesus Christ and by the Spirit of our God."

Matthew Henry makes three observations about these verses. First, God has put forth a plain truth that cannot be ignored—such sinners (vv 9, 10) will not inherit the kingdom of God. They shall not be considered true members of the church on earth, nor will they be admitted to the glorious church in heaven.

These sins are called life-dominating sins because they describe the very sin and person by that name. They represent who the person is, i.e., fornicator, idolater, adulterer, the effeminate or male prostitute, homosexual, thief, the covetous, drunkard, reviler, and swindler. These individuals shall not inherit the kingdom of God.

Second, Paul warns about deceiving ourselves. In speaking about verse 9, Matthew Henry says, "We cannot hope to sow to the flesh and yet reap eternal life."[15] We cannot live in sin and die in Christ. We cannot live the life of the devil's children and go to heaven with the children of God. This would be gross cheating, and cheating the soul leads to eternal damnation.

Third, the grace of God and His glorious Gospel make change possible. "And such were some of you" (v. 11 NASB). Those who were known by their wickedness were changed; they were different; they were not what they once were. They were washed and sanctified and justified in the name of the Lord. The vilest were changed into saints.

These sins which Paul names are indeed sins and not genetic problems, as some would suggest. "All the lifestyles mentioned here are sin-engendered. The hope lies in this: Jesus Christ died for sins, not for genetic problems. Call what the Bible calls 'sin', 'sin', and you will restore hope to many who have been led astray by modern propaganda."[16]

Women are looking for ways to circumvent the Scriptures by saying they are in a loving monogamous relationship, but 1 Corinthians 6:9 leaves no room for any form of homosexuality. They are being deceived and deceiving themselves.

In 1 Timothy 1:9, 10 Paul says that the law was made for the purpose of convicting sinners, not for condemning the righteous. " . . . the law is not made for a righteous man, but for those who are lawless and rebellious, for the ungodly and sinners, for the unholy and profane . . . and immoral men and homosexuals . . . and whatever else is contrary to sound teaching . . ." (NASB). Some would try to make the law support the way they are living, but that is entirely out of accord with the message of Scripture and the Biblical teaching of responsibility.

People have not basically changed over the centuries.

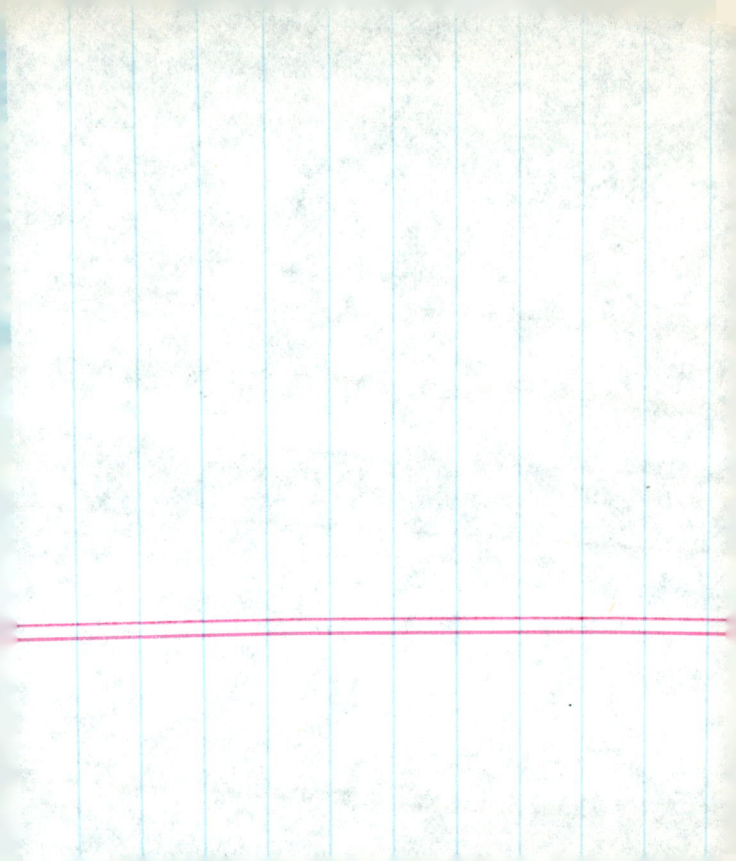

Paul wrote this letter to Timothy because the Jews were using the law unlawfully to divide the church, to cover up opposition to the Gospel, and to justify their sin. As in Paul's time, anything that restrains wicked people and puts a stop to their vices will be resisted. Leaders of our churches carry a serious responsibility to preach the truths of God to their people without exceptions. "Therefore, no Christian church that approves homosexual behavior among members (let alone allows homosexuals to be ordained) can truthfully profess to embrace the authority of Scripture. Homosexuality contaminates the community until discipline occurs, culminating in condemnation with removal or confession with restoration."[17]

The book of Jude confronts false teachers who use Christian liberties as license for immorality. These false teachers crept into the church unnoticed, and Jude warned of the seriousness of their teaching (v. 4). He found these issues so important, in fact, that he set aside what he had originally planned to write and addressed this growing problem (v. 3).

He warned that those who turn the grace of God into lasciviousness or license to sin "do in effect deny the Lord Jesus."[18] Jesus, in Mark 7:6, tells us that "This people honors me with their lips but their heart is far away from me." (NASB) False teaching may sound good and soothe some consciences, but it is not based on the Word of God and must be rejected.

When he speaks of godless, immoral men, Jude uses Sodom and Gomorrah as an example, and he urges those who are loved by Christ to not let the same thing cause their destruction. He tells them to contend earnestly for the faith. "Here 'faith' indicates the content of the message taught by the apostles and held in common by all Christians."[19]

What about the spiritually ignorant? It is always helpful to understand the background from which those in homosexuality have come. Some will have no spiritual background, and although their consciences have bothered them in the past, they have moved beyond that, have found other people who share similar desires, and have settled into the homosexual lifestyle. Where once they felt alone and perhaps isolated, they now feel part of a community.

Some are miserable living as they are, but since they have found no hope for change, they will try to accept themselves with "This is the way I am." They also will find a network of support.

Then, there are those who at one time believed homosexuality to be a sin but have changed their minds. They were devastated to realize they were tempted in this area and fought the temptation perhaps for years. In some cases counseling was sought. When these strong desires did not abate and, in their estimation, God did not answer their prayers for deliverance, they looked to soothe their consciences by finding a way to continue to live in sin by calling it another name. Perhaps their Christian upbringing made them want to hold on to Christ and at the same time find a way to continue in their homosexuality. Looking for a church that would not condemn their sin and somehow trying to bring the two things together became their goal. Sadly to say, there are such churches and groups that do just that—try to link homosexuality and Christianity together as though they are compatible.

So, not unlike the day in which Jude wrote, deception is everywhere, as are scoffers who follow their own ungodly desires, even in the church. Jude admonishes all of us to contend earnestly for the faith (v. 3) and build ourselves up in the most holy faith, praying to the Holy Spirit (v. 20).

Obviously Jude is pointing out sexual sin, and when he cites Sodom and Gomorrah as examples, he says their sin was gross immorality and strange flesh or perversion. The "strange flesh" in verse 7 is the homosexuality described in

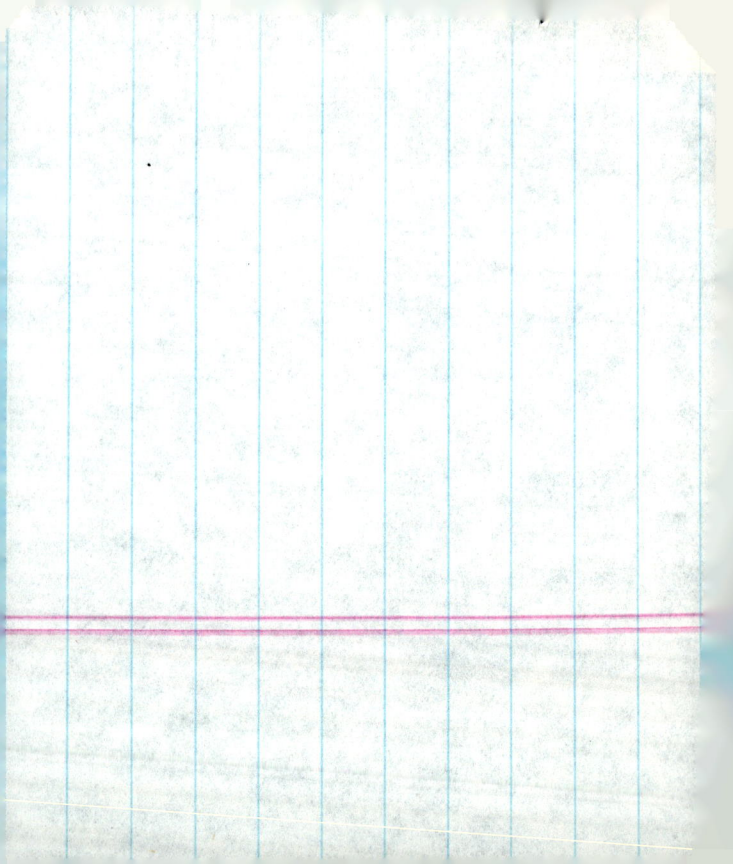

Genesis 19:4, 5. "They were guilty of abominable wickedness, not to be named or thought of but with the utmost abhorrence and detestation."[20] God does not change. "God is the same holy, just, pure Being now as then; and can the beastly pleasures of a moment make amends for your suffering the vengeance of eternal fire?"[21]

Revelation 21:8 warns that the sexually immoral, along with many others including murderers, idolaters, and liars, will have their part in the lake of fire. This cannot be any plainer.

The Old and New Testaments, from Genesis to Revelation, agree in their moral teachings. The Bible transcends what some say are cultural limitations. "Because God's holy character never changes, His moral law never changes. God is sovereign over culture, not subject to it. Society's changing values do not change God's moral law, which is valid for any and every culture regardless of its beliefs. ...we may conclude that if God's prohibitions against homosexuality were restricted to specific times or practices and no longer relevant, God would certainly have told us so in the New Testament."[22]

There is hope for men and women whose sexual desires are toward the same sex. That hope is found in God's Word which directs them to the person of the Lord Jesus Christ. John the Baptist referred to Jesus as the Lamb of God who takes away the sin of the world. When daughters come to Christ, He will enable them to live a life dominated by the work of the Holy Spirit rather than the sinful desires of homosexuality.

Leaving a life of sin and following Christ is what the Bible calls us to do. Putting off the sin of homosexuality is necessary because to do anything less is to come under God's judgment and condemnation. This putting off is possible because of what Peter tells us in 2 Peter 1:3, "His divine power has given us everything we need for life and godliness through our knowledge of Him who called us by His own glory and goodness."

In Matthew 11:28, Christ bids all who are weary and burdened to come to Him. He says His yoke is easy and His burden light, and compared to the immoral drives of this sinful behavior, it is. The Holy Spirit will walk alongside, helping in times of temptation. Second Timothy 2:19 says, "Everyone who confesses the name of the Lord must turn away from wickedness." We can be reassured that God never calls His children to do something they cannot possibly do. He does not require anything without providing the ability to do it. Joe Dallas, past president of Exodus International says, "... if someone as deluded as I was can be brought out of homosexuality, then surely anyone can."[23]

Along with hope comes responsibility. First Peter 1:13-15 admonishes us to guard our minds and exercise self-control, to hope in the grace God has given us, and to be holy as He is holy. To love God is to obey His commands. To say we know God and yet disregard clear directions about how to live is to lie. First John 2:6 says, "Whoever claims to live in Him must walk as Jesus did."

To doubt that the beloved daughter will ever come to Christ and give up her life in homosexuality is to say the power of our God is limited; but, that is not true, "For nothing is impossible with God" (Luke 1:37). These words were spoken to Mary about Elizabeth, the mother of John the Baptist. God granted Elizabeth, barren until old age, the ability to conceive, carry, and deliver a son. What seemed humanly impossible was made possible by God.

Homosexuality is a life-dominating sin, but it "... comes from the same heart that generates greed, envy, strife, disobedience to parents, and gossip" (Rom 1:29-32).[24]

As with any other sinner, the homosexual must be ministered to with humility, realizing that but for the grace of God, anyone of us could be deceived.

We are not talking about a disease or psychological disorder. We are talking about sin, and that gives great hope, for "The blood of Christ purifies us from all sin" (1 John 1:7). What about orientation? This word, like some other words regarding the homosexual movement, has taken on all flavors of new meanings. If someone thinks this is her orientation, might a different approach be appropriate? Well, the obvious fact is since the fall, all of mankind is oriented toward sinfulness in one way or another. Some express sinfulness in the form of greed, some in the form of jealousy, others in the form of homosexual desires. In his booklet *HOMOSEXUALITY*, Edward Welch has the following charts.[25] The first section shows the unbiblical concept of homosexuality; the second section shows the Biblical way homosexuality develops. The primary cause of homosexuality is a sinful heart.

Primary cause	Secondary cause	Response
Biology, or deficit in relationship with same-sex parent, low self-esteem, and so on	→ sin →	homosexuality

A Common, Unbiblical Conceptualization of the Development of Homosexuality

Primary Cause	Secondary Influences	Sinful Practice
Sinful heart	→ genetics, peer, family, sexual violation by an older person and so on	→ homosexuality

The Development of Homosexuality

Welch furthers points out that it is not what influences us from the outside but what comes from the inside. Mark 7:21-23 says, "For from within, out of men's hearts, come evil thoughts, sexual immorality, theft, murder, adultery, greed, malice, deceit, lewdness, envy, slander, arrogance and folly. All these evils come from inside and make a man unclean." Though outside influences may contribute to the direction one takes, they cannot be considered the primary sources according to the Scriptures. "Thus says the Lord, 'The heart is deceitful above all things and desperately wicked'" (Jer 17:5a, 9a NKJV).

King David knew that his heart was bent toward evil, and in Psalm 51:10, he cried for God to create in him a pure heart. In Psalm 86:11, he asked for an undivided heart. He wanted his allegiance to be only to God. Proverbs 4:23 says, "Above all else, guard your heart, for it is the wellspring of life."

Another natural progression of the depraved human heart is that humanity, men and women, become idol worshippers. Something becomes an idol when it is wanted so badly that a person is willing to sin in order to get it. Anything that comes before God, separates you from Him. Isaiah 59:2 tells us, "But your iniquities have separated you from your God; your sins have hidden His face from you." Our deepest problem is our idolatrous hearts. Our idols include pleasure, control, comfort, and personal gratification. Our idols center around us—we are loyal to ourselves. When a choice between pleasing ourselves and pleasing God confronts us, we always find it easier to choose self over God.

Many people would agree that idolatry was a major problem in the Old Testament. Over and over, Israel was told to remove their "high places" and get rid of their false gods. Today, the second commandment is thought to be the one commandment least broken. However, the writers of the New Testament speak often of the sin of idolatry.

In Colossians 3:5, Paul exhorts, "Put to death, therefore,

whatever belongs to your earthly nature: sexual immorality, impurity, lust, evil desires and greed, which is idolatry." First Corinthians 10:14 says we are to flee from idolatry. In the last verse of 1 John, John's imperative is, "Dear children, keep yourselves from idols." Several Scriptures reveal God as a jealous God. Exodus 34:14 says, "Do not worship any other god, for the LORD, whose name is Jealous, is a jealous God." God simply will not share first place in the heart. Anything that rivals God must be put to death.

In Ephesians 2, Paul reminded the Ephesians that they were once dead in their trespasses and sin, gratifying the cravings of their sinful nature and following its desires and thoughts. Now, through God's mercy, they are made alive and created to do good works. God, who is rich in mercy makes permanent changes. He is the only hope for those struggling with the sin of homosexuality.

See Appendixes B, C, D

CHAPTER V

UNBIBLICAL VIEWS REFUTED

∞

The homosexual community has its own ways of interpreting Scripture, therefore, ministering to them is a challenge. The meanings for some passages of Scripture, which have always seemed clear, have been interpreted differently. "Homosexuals have their own identity, culture, socialization process, and theories of knowledge. What seems Biblically straightforward to many Christians might be understood very differently by the homosexual."[26] The words "sin" and "disobedience" may not have the same meaning. Whereas the Bible is the final authority to the Christian, the homosexual may appeal to feelings and rights.

"Jesus did not condemn the practice of homosexuality" is the statement often heard when a daughter wants to justify her lifestyle. This statement does not indicate His approval or acceptance either, and if we were to make a list of other things Jesus did not address, incest, bestiality and rape would have to be included. The more important issue here is, Jesus would not have approved of something that is forbidden in the Old Testament, nor would He have disregarded all the mores of His Jewish culture.

When teaching about the male and female relationship, Jesus says, "Haven't you read . . . that at the beginning the Creator 'made them male and female,' . . . and the two will become one flesh" (Matt 19:4, 5). "The emphatic terms *male* and *female* (arsen and thelys) are used here rather than simply *man* and *woman* (aner and gynee). This and the nature of the expression imply exclusiveness of categories, that is these two and no other forms."[27]

Jesus' reference to Sodom, His teachings on the nature of marriage, and His handling of the righteous standards of the Law point to His condemnation of this sexual practice. More than any other teacher, Jesus mentions Sodom and the events surrounding its destruction.[28]

At any point in His ministry, Jesus could have included same-sex relationships, saying that the principles under discussion also apply to their sexual union, but He did not. If people are "born" homosexuals, Jesus could have called their desires natural and given them principles and guidelines, but He did not. Nowhere in the Gospels or in all of Scripture is there found the slightest hint that homosexuality is an acceptable lifestyle. In every place it is condemned and called detestable—an abomination. In one place only does Jesus refer to a possible alternative to marriage and that is celibacy (Matt 19:12).

"God destroyed Sodom because the people were inhospitable" is another statement the homosexual will use as the reason for God's judgment. In 1954, Derrick Bailey, a modern theologian, issued a call to reinterpret this passage, saying no reference to homosexuality could be supported. He contends that when "know" is used in Genesis 19 it means the men wanted to get acquainted with the strangers. He further argues that "know" (*yada*, in Greek) appears 943 times in the Old Testament and very few of those times have a sexual connotation.[29] However, when a word has more than one meaning, the crucial factor is context, not how frequently it is used.

An understanding of hermeneutics is essential to everyone who approaches the Bible for understanding and correct interpretation. Hermeneutics is the science and art of interpretation. Proper interpretation must use methods, techniques, and rules to determine a true interpretation; therefore, no one is free to interpret any Scripture without giving careful attention to these guidelines.

If these careful guidelines are not followed, inaccurate interpretations will be made, mistakes leading to disobedience are sure to occur, and rationalizing why certain principles do not apply will be used to soothe an otherwise pricked conscience. Emotions will replace conviction, and the heart will become hardened.

The homosexual community does not want to acknowledge the Bible's teaching concerning their particular sin. They read the words, and they see the necessity to explain them away because they are so clear. This cannot be done easily with Genesis 19. The context demands a recognition of the intent of the men who demanded to "know" these strangers. If it had not been sexual in nature, Lot would not have offered his daughters, calling attention to their virginity.

To continue their argument about "inhospitality", revisionists go to Jesus' words when He speaks of Sodom's destruction in Matthew 10:14,15 and Luke 10:10-12. They say Jesus' point is that if people do not welcome the disciples into their towns (are inhospitable), they are to leave. The main thrust of this passage of Scripture, however, is missed. In the preceding verses, Jesus is talking about a message the disciples were to deliver to the towns. The 70, sent out by the Lord, were sent out with the message of repentance. Their message was that the kingdom of heaven was near and the people needed to repent. God's condemnation was because the people rejected the message of Christ, not because they were inhospitable.

Another Scripture that signifies the primary sin of Sodom was sexual in nature is 2 Peter 2:7-10. Peter, referring to the men in Sodom, says that Lot was distressed by the filthy lives of lawless men ("sensual conduct of unprincipled men," v. 7, NASB). Verse 9 tells us that God will hold the unrighteous for judgment—the unrighteous being those who follow the corrupt desire of their sinful nature (v. 10).

Jude carries the same interpretation when he refers to Sodom. The lack of hospitality did not bring down the wrath of God; it was gross immorality. "Just as Sodom and Gomorrah and the cities around them, since they in the same way as these indulged in gross immorality and went after strange flesh, are exhibited as an example in undergoing the punishment of eternal fire" (v. 7, NASB). "Jude serves as a lesson and a divine warning to all men and women in homosexuality."[30]

"None of the passages will sustain the view that the sin involved at Sodom or Gibeah was merely inhospitality or violence; none of the texts cites inhospitality. Revisionist attempts to use patristic interpretations fail. The church fathers simply do not support these arguments."[31]

The destruction of Sodom shows God's utter disdain for that which takes its name from the city - sodomy. Sodom, which in c. 2065 B.C. was fertile and populous "...is now a burnt-out region of oil and asphalt."[32] Its ruins, which were still visible until the first century A.D., are now buried under the slowly rising water of the Salt Sea.

"The references to sexual relations in Leviticus 18 and 20 do not apply to us today because they are part of the obsolete Old Testament ceremonial laws," is also argued. This argument is also flawed; first of all, because this is speaking of moral laws rather than ceremonial laws and second, because it carries with it a more severe penalty when compared to the breaking of either the civil or ceremonial laws.

Among several laws spelled out in the Old Testament are the civil law, the ceremonial law, and the moral law. The civil law dealt with things including restitution, marriage and divorce, slavery, business transactions, finances, and dealings with the poor. The ceremonial law gave instructions for ceremonies of worship; e.g., clean and unclean animals, the handling of the dead, and which animals to use for which ceremony, to name a few.

There are actions, however, that have nothing to do with how a society functions or with how ceremonies are maintained. "They are commonly stated in categorical imperatives, and the punishment, when prescribed, is death. They are thus viewed as offenses against God or against life itself."[33] Homosexual acts, sin under the moral law, are ". . . prohibited because they grow out of and lead to a world view that is radically opposed to that of the Bible. They are prohibited because they deny the creation order of God and thus the very nature of God Himself."[34] These activities are produced by the world's philosophy which denies boundaries. "It is a philosophy that denies transcendence with its teachings of firm boundaries between God and His creation and between various parts of that creation."[35] Homosexuality is not prohibited because of civil or ceremonial reasons but because it is a moral offense.

"What is referred to as being abominable in Levitcus is idolatry, not homosexuality," is another false statement. Still another, "God does not prohibit homosexuality as we see it today." Prohomosexual authors say homosexuality, in and of itself, is not a sin. Homosexuality associated with idolatry or its practice as part of idol worship is the sin.

Among the many sins listed in these chapters of Leviticus, including homosexuality, are incest, adultery, and bestiality. To say homosexuality is wrong only when it is associated with idolatry would mean all the other activities are sinful only when they are a part of idolatry. "Given the generally negative attitudes toward homosexual acts common in places such as Egypt, Assyria and Babylon, it would be completely out of character for the Old Testament law to prohibit homosexuality associated with idol worship while permitting it for other purposes."[36]

There are numerous unbiblical views touted as reasons homosexuality would not be condemned by God, but we will consider one last one. That one has to do with the terms "natural" and "unnatural" and the idea of orientation. The Christian would define "unnatural," in this context, as any sexual activity other than what God designed between a male and female. Paul said homosexuality was "against nature," or against what God intended from the beginning. "In the New Testament, the 'natural' pertains to the created world and its present general order as ordained by God . . . (His) creation ordinance, with the specific distinction between male and female, intended for heterosexual relations to be 'natural'."[37] Anything else is a perversion of God's created order.

The homosexual community interprets "natural" and "unnatural" quite differently; e.g., homosexuality is as "natural" to the homosexual as the dominance of the left hand is to a left-handed person. Since a person does not choose to be left-handed or homosexual, it is "natural" to them. They conclude that homosexuality is wrong and "unnatural" only when a heterosexual practices it because it would be against her nature. In other words, it is sinful for a heterosexual to practice homosexuality but not for a homosexual to do so.

This argument is used when someone says she was "born that way." But the same argument can be used for a rapist or a pedophile—they cannot help it, they were born that way. How absurd to believe that the Scriptures on drunkenness do not apply to the drunkard because he is an alcoholic or the Scriptures on stealing do not apply to the thief because he is a kleptomaniac.

The belief that people are born with a genetic predisposition toward homosexuality (or as some say, with a homosexual orientation) is held by many today. However, when sexologist, Alfred Kinsey, took a survey of homosexuals in the 1940s, and asked them how they got to be "gay," only nine percent said, "I was born gay." In 1970, the percentage was nearly the same, but in 1983, the percent rose to 22 and then to 35 percent in 1990. This is very significant because if only one-third of those living in homosexuality believe "God made me this way," how is it that many heterosexuals believe it? And many do. Actually, in any of the studies or medical research done over the years, homosexuality has not been proven to be either genetic or biological in its origin.

Society, more and more, finds itself confused about truth without the Bible as the basis for life. Some find, "It is politically expedient to view sexual orientation as inborn; many people who would otherwise consider homosexuality immoral will support gay rights if they can be convinced it is an inherited trait."[38]

The homosexual community has tried for years to desensitize the peoples of the world by flooding every sector of society with propaganda favoring acceptance of their sin. Because of their efforts, people are questioning the possibility of this being an inbred biological condition. "The implications of their view are that because the homosexual cannot change, all aspects of society must change instead, including education, religion, and the law."[39]

The Word of God cannot be twisted to allow for homosexuality under any circumstances. If the liberty is taken to do so, then nothing prevents anyone from doing the same thing with the other 14 sins listed in the last verses of Romans 1. Under what circumstances might it be considered all right to be greedy, malicious, or to invent evil? The excuses "I was born that way" or "It is just my nature" will not work. The sin of homosexuality must be dealt with just as with all other sin—through coming to Christ in repentance, being granted forgiveness, and daily dying to self and living for God. "If homosexuality could gain divine approval in any sense, Paul would have indicated as much and drawn the distinctions which men now wish to impose upon his text. Scripture cannot be interpretively shaped to fit the contours of sin, and homosexuality cannot be cleverly domesticated within a divinely approved lifestyle."[40]

The Scriptures tell us that since the fall of Adam and Eve in the garden of Eden, all men and women have an orientation toward sin. Parents do not have to teach their children to be selfish or rebellious; yet they are. Some of the first words a child learns are "mine" and "no." From where do these responses come? They come from our fallen nature, for in Adam we all died spiritually (1 Cor 15:22). Out of our sinful nature comes corrupt desires (2 Pet 2:10) and lustful desires (2 Pet 2:18). First John 2:16 says that the cravings of sinful man, or the lust of the flesh, comes not from the Father but from the world. Blaming God for making a homosexual is refuted very clearly in this passage.

First Peter 2:11 admonishes us to abstain from sinful desires or fleshly lusts because they wage war against the soul. Galatians 5:17 tells us that, ". . . the sinful nature desires what is contrary to the Spirit, and the Spirit what is contrary to the sinful nature." This applies to areas in the lives of everyone. Some people seem to "have been born" with an uncanny ability to lie and "get off with it." They never seem to get caught. Some people battle jealousy in their lives and are unable to rejoice with those who rejoice. For some it is envy; some find it hard to control anger.

When homosexuality is classified in the sin category, as the Bible classifies it, there is both hope and great fear. Galatians 5:19-20 says, "The acts of the sinful nature are obvious: sexual immorality, impurity and debauchery . . .

discord, jealousy, fits of rage, selfish ambition . . . drunkenness . . . and the like." Hope comes from crucifying the sinful nature by repenting and being forgiven. The fear lies in continuing to live to please the sinful nature. "I warn you, as I did before, that those who live like this will not inherit the kingdom of God" (Gal 5:21b). If the Apostle Paul had approved a homosexual orientation, he would have had to violate what God, in His own image, created; i.e., "Only a monogamous union of male and female constitutes marriage on the Maker's model (Matt. 19:1-19). Homosexual orientation violates the nature and law of this Creator and reflects the fall of Genesis 3."[41] Not only does it violate God's holy law, it represents a departure into abomination and is dishonorable and degrading. It will, along with all other life-dominating sins, come under God's judgment and wrath.

"The deception of homosexual orientation must be exposed and corrected. It is a false teaching that will eventually lead to bad fruit. We truly do have an 'orientation,' but it is a spiritual orientation that is against God. It is not a simple physical inclination."[42]

Calling homosexuality a sin is not a violation of the homosexual's dignity as a person, as some claim. It is because of a person's dignity, made in the image of God, that we must disapprove of this sin.[43] God's condemnation comes down upon all who deviate from heterosexual monogamy. There is an absolute standard for sexuality set forth in the Word of God, and anyone departing from it stands in direct opposition to God and stand to be the object of His wrath.

CHAPTER VI

SHARING THE BURDEN

∞

In 1 Corinthians 10:13, God promises to not put on His people more than they can bear. He will always be faithful. One way God helps His people in times of distress is through the support and prayers of other Christians. Parents will be faced immediately and in the future with decisions regarding disclosure. Whom should they tell and why and how much? Grieving parents will actually want no one to know about their daughter. They will want to withdraw from activities for fear of giving away their "secret" or appearing as though something is wrong and then having to explain it. They will face many awkward moments. They will become experts at evading direct questions concerning their daughter. They will learn to live, as it were, with their guard up. They will experience a sick feeling whenever the subject of homosexuality is mentioned. Shame, because of the daughter's choice of lifestyle or who might be the blame, is part of every day. Life becomes uncomfortable.

The Scriptures exhort Christians to carry one another's burdens. Yet, many parents choose to conceal these burdens and not allow anyone the privilege of helping them. They know Christians are to rejoice with those who rejoice and weep with those who weep, but their pride and shame keep them from seeking help.

The daughter's choice to live the homosexual lifestyle will remain a secret only so long. Parents again ask many questions. Could my pride be standing in the way of sharing with fellow believers? What will people think of me and my family? Will people wonder about how we reared our children? Could friendships be lost because of this? What will people say? Will they talk behind our backs? The questions are endless.

When the decision is made to ask someone for prayer, with whom is it safe to share such devastating information? It is always safe to share the concerns with mature, loving, and praying believers who will hold in confidence what you have shared and at the same time pray fervently for the daughter and the family. The information is not shared just to inform. It is shared for the purpose of prayer and encouragement. If the daughter has sworn Mom and Dad to secrecy, which is unwise, they will need to go to her and tell her of their decision to speak to the pastor, an elder, or a trusted friend. They should explain to her that their sole purpose is to have people pray. If the daughter has come out with her homosexuality and does not seem to care who knows, of course, this will not be necessary.

What about telling younger siblings? Factors to be considered are age and maturity of the children and whether or not the homosexual family member lives at home and is open with her homosexuality.[44]

Careful consideration should be given to the other family members because if they know something is wrong and are not informed as to what it is, they may conclude that Mom and Dad are having marital problems and are contemplating a divorce. Since sensitive siblings may feel ignored, they may think the parents are withdrawing from them, and they may become disruptive in their behavior.

Sin does not affect only the person doing the sinning, but it also affects the entire family, the church, and anyone who cares and loves this particular individual. The Apostle Paul talks about the body of Christ, meaning the church, and says, "If one part suffers, every part suffers with it . . ." (1 Cor 12:26).

What these trusted friends and church leaders should know is a logical question. Telling someone on your own volition is easier than being put on the spot because you can plan what to say and how much to tell. When someone asks specific questions, the task is harder. The answer might simply be, "She needs your prayers." If more information is sought and you know the person is truly concerned and has a desire to pray, you might devulge more. Details are not as important as saying, "She is not following the Lord right now, nor is she being obedient to His Word." It is very difficult to say, "She is living in the homosexual lifestyle," but it may be necessary to do so. The Lord will give you wisdom if you are striving to please Him with every conversation. James gives this reminder in James 1:5, "If any of you lacks wisdom, he should ask God, who gives generously to all without finding fault, and it will be given him." God knows that these trying times are difficult, and He is willing to come alongside and be with His children every moment of every day.

The Bible has many examples of people in great need and of those who helped by coming alongside. Naomi and Ruth shared joy, then sorrow, then joy. They bore the burden of seeking a new life after both their husbands died. They helped one another. David and Jonathan remained friends and supported each other in terribly dangerous times. God used Jonathan to spare David's life. Paul and Silas suffered together. They were imprisoned, where, instead of getting depressed, they prayed and sang hymns to the glory of God. All through Paul's life, he solicited the prayers of God's people. He also reached out to others, and when he was bidding farewell to the Ephesian elders, he reminded them that for three years, with tears, he had ministered to them. These serve as examples today that we may follow in times of need.

CHAPTER VII

EFFECTIVE PRAYER IN DIFFICULT TIMES

∽

"The effective prayer of a righteous man can accomplish much" (Jas 5:16b NASB). "The effectual fervent prayer of a righteous man avails much" (Jas 6:16b NKJV).

Sometimes all you can do is pray. The phrase, "All you can do is pray," does not mean that when all else fails, pray. It does not mean you should do nothing else but pray. It does mean that when no amount of talking has been persuasive, and the more you talk the greater the distance grows between parents and daughter, it is time to put most of your effort into prayer. It does not mean that you will never again say another word on the subject either, but to plow and replow the same ground produces nothing of value.

Prayer for the daughter's salvation is first and foremost. When she tries to convince you of her love for Christ and yet continues to be dominated by this sin, or if she repents and falls into it again and is truly doing battle with this particular sin, other very specific prayers may be offered to God. Pray that God will send a strong Christian friend into her life who

...not be afraid to remind her, with Scripture, that she is not living to please the Lord. Pray that she will be receptive.

The most often prayed prayers are that the Lord would break up the current relationship, make the daughter miserable in her sin, take sleep away until she repents, etc. There certainly is nothing wrong with praying those prayers, but perhaps following the principles of Ephesians 4: 22-24 would be more Biblical and far more productive. Those verses say, "You were taught, with regard to your former way of life, to put off your old self, which is being corrupted by its deceitful desires; to be made new in the attitude of your minds; and to put on the new self, created to be like God in true righteousness and holiness." Jay Adams, in his commentary says, "Change is a two-factored process. Putting off will not be permanent without putting on." Ephesians 4:25 says, " . . . each of you must put off falsehood and speak truthfully . . . " and Ephesians 4:28 says, "He who has been stealing must steal no longer, but must work . . . that he may have something to share with those in need."

Instead of always asking the Lord to take away homosexual desires or break up relationships, pray that He will replace them. Using this "put off" and "put on" principle, change your prayer and your focus to, "Lord, replace the heart of stone with a heart of flesh. Replace the desire to please self with the desire to please God. Replace the love my daughter has for herself with a deep love for You. Replace the delusional ideas of Scripture and the misinterpretations with true Biblical understanding. Reveal the deception and replace it with truth and honesty. Replace the human desire with godly desire. Replace fear with trust. Replace loneliness with Your presence. Replace the insecurity with 'God is my refuge and strength'. Replace selfishness with a desire to die to self. Replace the acts to just soothe the conscience with obedience to God's Word. Change the focus of herself to a focus on Christ and others.

Replace this present relationship with a God-honoring relationship. Replace the busyness of filling every waking moment, with times of reflection and assessment. Help her to see her sin as You see it. May it become as abominable to her as it is to You."

The following prayer has been helpful to parents whose daughter has bought into the sin of homosexuality. With its emphasis on Scripture, it has been a tool to use when words are hard to find. It can be prayed from the heart as the words are based on the Word of God. The daughter's name can fill in the blanks which make it a very personal prayer to the Lord.

BONDAGE BREAKING PRAYER

"Father, we come boldly to Your throne of grace, and find mercy and grace to help in time of need. Grant _____ release from bondage to strongholds of the enemy. We plead the blood of Jesus to cancel all commands of the powers of darkness in _____'s life. Jesus came to destroy the works of the devil. His blood defeated the god of this age. In Jesus' name, take back all ground _____ gave the enemy. Draw _____ out of bondage and deception.

We have the heavenly intercession of the Holy Spirit and Jesus. Father, focus the intercession of the Spirit on _____. Answer these prayers according to Your perfect will. Lord Jesus, our Intercessor, apply all Your mighty work against the enemy. Bring all the power of the incarnation, crucifixion, resurrection, and ascension against the assignments seeking to destroy _____. Most High God, contend with those who contend with _____. Rebuke the enemy in all his operations. Dispatch mighty warrior angels to do battle on _____'s behalf.

Send Your light and Your truth and lead _____. Remove all spiritual blindness, deafness, and hardness of heart. Grant _____ eyes to see, ears to hear, and a heart that seeks You. Bind a hedge of thorns around _____ that will repel all the works of darkness in _____'s life.

This battle is not against flesh and blood, and we have spiritual weapons that set captives free. By Your Holy Spirit, break every yoke of bondage in _____'s life. Grant _____conviction of sin with godly sorrow to repentance and deliverance from captivity. Set _____ completely free. It is written, you shall know the truth and the Truth shall set you free. We overcome by the blood of the Lamb and by the word of our testimony. Thank You for Your mighty work by the blood of Christ Jesus. Thank You for granting me the grace, power, persistence, and love in intercession with faith for _____ until You are glorified in _____life. In Jesus' name, Amen."

Adapted and abridged from "The Adversary"
by Mark Bubeck.[45]

A. W. Pink expounds upon the importance of prayer when he says, "...prayer *redounds to God's glory,* for in prayer we do but acknowledge our dependency upon Him. In the second place, prayer is appointed by God *for our spiritual blessing,* as a means for *our growth in grace.* Third, prayer is appointed by God for our seeking from Him the things which we are in need of."[46]

Prayer is not to inform God of problems and spell out to Him the daughter's sin because He already knows what she needs even before the request is made (Matt 6:8). So why pray? First, we are commanded to pray. Jesus told us what to pray for and, by His example, how to pray. In Luke 18:1, Jesus says to pray always and not give up. First Thessalonians 5:17 tells us to pray continually. Second, prayer is more then supplication; it is communion that includes adoration, confession, and thanksgiving.

Prayer is the means with which God brings about His eternal decrees. Prayer does not change God's purposes, for what He has decreed will come to pass. Again, prayer's purpose is not to alter God's plan but to accomplish it in His way and in His time. God is not standing by to do our bidding, granting to us what we think is needed. "No, prayer is a coming to God, telling Him my *need*, committing my way unto the Lord, and leaving Him to deal with it as seemeth *Him* best."[47]

More than asking, prayer is an attitude of dependency. It is a declaration of our weaknesses. It is the acknowledgment of our utter dependence on God, a submission to His Divine will, and a confidence that what He chooses for us is best.

Understanding the place of prayer will help parents to continue to pray for their daughter month after month and year after year when their relationship with her continues to deteriorate and how she lives is unchanged. A true understanding of prayer encourages parents to recognize God's sovereignty and reminds them that often our ways are not God's ways, nor is our timing His timing. It is a lesson in patience and trust in the loving God.

A word of caution—Christian parents will spend many hours in prayer for the daughter living in homosexuality and often neglect to pray for their other children, their spouse, and other members of the family and church family. There is a tendency to be so consumed with her and her sin that the prayer time is just about her. There is no question that daily seeking the face of God for this daughter is important, but to be so consumed as to neglect others is wrong. Philippians 4:6 reminds us about anxiety when it says, "Do not be anxious about anything, but in everything by prayer and petition, with thanksgiving, present your requests to God." Verse 7 of the same chapter says, "And the peace of God, which transcends all understanding, will guard your hearts and your minds in Christ Jesus."

"A parent must pray for his children. Monica, the mother of Augustine, prayed for his conversion, and someone said it was impossible that a son of so many prayers and tears should perish. The soul of your child is in a snare and will you not pray that it may 'recover out of the snare of the devil' (2 Tim. 2:26)? Many parents are careful to lay up portions for their children, but they do not lay up prayers for them."[48]

It is encouraging to know that both Jesus, and the Holy Spirit, are interceding before the Father on behalf of His children (Rom 8:26, 34). Parents do not have to carry the burden alone but can call upon the Triune God to sustain them in the darkest of times.

CHAPTER VIII

STRAINED RELATIONSHIPS

∾

As long as a daughter chooses to give in to the sin of homosexuality, the relationship between her and her God-fearing parents will be strained. Words, no matter how innocently spoken, will be judged and misjudged. She will accuse her parents of not wanting to understand. She will be defensive. Parents, too, may become defensive and not speak as gently as they should. Parents will be misunderstood no matter how carefully they think through a conversation and word it with extreme caution. The truth is, the daughter and her parents are living, as it were, on parallel lines—lines that never meet. They are walking in opposite directions toward very different goals. What is important to one is not important to the other.

Attitudes, ideas, interests, and goals are now very different. The parents believe in the clear teaching about homosexuality as seen in Scripture. The daughter looks for ways to reinterpret, revise, and explain them away. The once easy discussions of Biblical truths are now areas in which this is heard: "That is just your interpretation. There are others." The family unit, which used to be so important and still is to the parents, has been traded for a "new family" by the daughter—one that understands and does not condemn. Places where everyone enjoyed going together are no longer of interest to the daughter, and the places in which the daughter now feels comfortable are uncomfortable to the parents. An invisible wall continues to separate the two.

Luke 12:51-53 says, "Do you think I came to bring peace on earth? No, I tell you, but division. From now on there will be five in one family divided against each other, three against two and two against three. They will be divided, father against son and son against father, mother against daughter and daughter against mother..." The effect of the gospel will bring division."[49] The design of the gospel is to unite and knit together in love, but when it is opposed and rejected, it does the opposite. According to Luke 12 and Matthew 10, division will reach even into private families and bring discord among the nearest of relatives. "The one that continues in unbelief will be provoked, and will hate and persecute the one that by his faith and obedience witnesses against, and condemns, his unbelief and disobedience."[50] Matthew 10:35 tells us that a daughter will be against her mother because the Sword of the Spirit brings that division.

When the daughter insists that her living in homosexuality is not a sin, and therefore is not condemned by God, she is deceiving herself and is trying to appease her conscience. In truth, she knows the fellowship with her godly parents has been broken, and she knows why.

Paul asks a rhetorical question in 2 Corinthians 6:14, 15a. "For what do righteousness and wickedness have in common? Or what fellowship can light have with darkness? What harmony is there between Christ and Belial?" Herein lies the answer to why attitudes have changed and the once-close relationship is no longer there. One party is serving the Lord, obeying His commands and bringing glory to God. The other party has chosen to yield to the temptations of the flesh, and has disregarded the commands of Scripture. Therefore meaningful fellowship, as the Bible defines fellowship, is impossible. First John 1:7 tells us that those who are pure before God, because of the blood of Jesus, will have fellowship with one another. First John 2:4 warns that those who say they know Christ but disobey His commands are liars.

Activities will be curtailed. Since the wayward daughter is probably not living at home and perhaps not even in the same town, doing things together may be at a minimum. The tough times are holidays and special dates; e.g., birthdays and anniversaries. The daughter, very often, will have excuses as to why getting together is "next to impossible." Very often the parents, one or the other, or both, may not think the result is worth the effort. For the first several times, they may get together and try to recreate holidays past, but both parties only endure the time and part with a sigh of relief. After awhile, both sides wonder if they should even keep trying. Parents often leave with a heavy heart, wondering if things will ever change. Daughters leave with a sense of a duty fulfilled.

It is at these times that the Word of God can mightily minister to those seeking to do His will. Psalm 34:18 says, "The Lord is close to the brokenhearted and saves those who are crushed in spirit." Parents can identify with David in Psalm 3. David is fleeing from Absalom, calling him his foe. Daughters and parents are foes; they rise up against one another and hurts become a way of life. Continuing on, Psalm 3:3 has these words, "But you are a shield around me, O Lord; You bestow glory on me and lift up my head." In verse 4, David cries out to the Lord, and in verse 8 acknowledges that " . . . from the Lord comes deliverance." Verse 15 of Psalm 34 says, "The eyes of the Lord are on the righteous and his ears are attentive to their cry." Parents are not alone; the Holy Spirit is a constant companion.

At times, there will be long periods with little or no communication. It is, however, important to stay in contact. Telephone calls may be the hardest because their very nature demands a response, but there is mail and e-mail. This daughter, no doubt, will experience some very low times. In spite of what she says, all is not "gay". When the daughter calls home crying, and it will happen, because her latest relationship has broken up and her heart is broken, parents need the help of the Lord to even know what to say and how to respond. One couple stated that after their daughter and friend split up, they (the parents) tried to be as comforting as possible but at the same time were glad it had happened. Their hope was that this breakup would cause their daughter to come in repentance to Christ. This does not seem to be the best time to try again to evangelize the daughter. Waiting a few days may be much better. What to say is very difficult, and it is not like comforting a daughter whose boyfriend has left her. Saying that perhaps the Lord has someone else for her would mean different things to the two sides. The best advice, if she will listen, is to point her to Christ and His redemptive work and the comfort He gives to those who desire to please Him. Unless true repentance takes place, another relationship will develop, and the cycle begins all over again.

Ungodly attitudes, a lack of meaningful activities, and little to no interaction will produce a strained relationship between the daughter and her parents. Hurts will be deeply felt and frustrations will abound. If parents do not guard their hearts, they will find it easy to allow circumstances to rob them of their joy in the Lord. Rejoicing in the Lord will seem all but impossible.

Rejoicing in the Lord, however, is not about being happy because everything is going well. True rejoicing in the Lord during difficult times is about knowing God loves His children with an everlasting love and is directing everything according to His divine will. Paul's final instructions as he closed out his first letter to the Thessalonians include, "Be joyful always; pray continually; give thanks in all circumstances, for this is God's will for you in Christ Jesus (1 Thess 5:16-18). Making this a part of your walk with God is possible only when you understand the "how," as seen in verse 24: "The One who calls you is faithful and He will do it." When reading 1 Thessalonians 5:16-18, always include verse 24.

CHAPTER IX

SPIRITUAL GROWTH THROUGH TRIAL

∽

How does a father and mother sort out what has happened to their daughter? How do they even begin to understand the effects sin is having on members of the immediate and extended family? Where is God in all of this?

The life of Joseph, found in Genesis 37-50, may be the most encouraging account recorded in all of Scripture. Joseph was hurt deeply by family members who turned against him in the most wicked way. They even tried to kill him. From a young age, Joseph had difficulties in his life and was misunderstood. He began to be hated by his brothers when he reported their evil doings to their father. It is thought by Biblical scholars that Joseph's reporting was not done to be malicious, self-serving, or to sow discord, but because he thought his brothers would take the reproof and restrain themselves. The brothers took offense and hated him all the more.

Joseph was also hated by his brothers because he was his father's favorite son. Jacob favored Joseph because he was a son of his old age, and he was born to Rachel, the wife Jacob loved. Jacob did not hide his affection for Joseph and when he made Joseph a colorful coat, he exacerbated the already volatile relationship between the brothers.

Joseph's two dreams and the implications of both so infuriated his brothers that they decided to put an end to his badgering. They plotted to kill the dreamer. God, however, had other plans and used Reuben and Judah to spare Joseph's life. Instead of killing him, the brothers decided to sell him and did so to some Midianite merchants. The Midianites, in turn, sold Joseph in Egypt to Potiphar, an official of Pharaoh. All this transpired under the sovereignty of God.

Through no fault of his own, Joseph's life had been radically changed, and he had been separated from those he loved. Where was God? Genesis 39:2 tells us, "The Lord was with Joseph." When you delight in serving the Lord, and despite all efforts to do the right thing, you find yourself facing heartache or disappointment and are confused as to what to do, and when you wonder where God is in all of it, the answer is, "The Lord is with you."

Joseph found favor with Potiphar and was put in charge of his royal household. God blessed everything that was under Joseph's care. In the eyes of the world, this young man, Joseph, "had made it." Even though he had had a tough time at home, he now "had it all together." The story does not end here, however. Joseph, even though he was honest and faithful to his duties, once again faced trouble and trouble of the gravest kind. Potiphar's wicked wife lied about him, and he ended up in prison for a number of years. Where was God now? Genesis 39:21 says, "The Lord was with him."

Joseph was shown kindness in prison and was once again put in a place of authority. Genesis 39:23 says, "The Lord was with Joseph and gave him success in what-ever he did." After interpreting the cupbearer's dream, where the cupbearer was restored to his duties, Joseph experienced yet another disappointment. The cupbearer forgot "to put a good word in" about him. He was forgotten, but not by God.

God continued to be with Joseph and two years later, because he was able to interprete Pharaoh's dream, God restored him. When Joseph advised Pharaoh about how to plan for the upcoming seven-year famine, Pharaoh chose him to head the operation. God was with Joseph during the years of plenty and the years of famine. He was with Joseph when his brothers came for food and when he was finally reunited with his father and brother. God had a plan for Joseph's life, and his education, brought about by the sovereignty of God in the things he experienced, was directed by God Himself.

God was able to use Joseph to save the Egyptian nation and also His own people, the Israelites. Joseph would not have had the ability to plan for and withstand the opposition and pressures without the lessons he learned from his brothers' hatred of him, the experience of running a household, of dealing with injustices, and his being thrown into prison and forgotten. God's hand was on Joseph as it is on all who seek to do His will. The years of heartache and trials, whether in Joseph's life or yours, are not wasted. God is in control. He is not wringing His hand wondering what to do when your daughter continues to disobey and disregard His commands as stated in the Scriptures. So, what is He doing?

A correct view of God will stabilize every Christian in every circumstance where life does not, make sense, when those most dear have become strangers, when what used to work does not, and when seemingly hopeless situations leave one floundering around for answers. It is belief in the sovereignty of God that releases anxiety and allows Christians to live a life fully trusting God for themselves and their family during the most troubling times.

God does not always choose to reveal to His children the

reasons He does what He does, plans what He plans, or allows what He allows. "The sovereignty of the God of Scripture is absolute, irresistible, infinite . . .we affirm His right to govern the universe . . . His right is the right of the Potter over the clay . . . He is under no rule or law outside His own will and nature . . .He is under no obligation to give an account of His matters to any."[51]

The sovereignty of God is not always apparent. It is easy to believe in God's sovereignty when life is going smoothly. It is quite another thing when people do things that directly affect us. "...to believe in the sovereignty of God when we do not *see* His direct intervention - when God is, so to speak, working entirely behind the scenes through ordinary circumstances and ordinary actions of people - is even more important because that is the way God usually works."[52]

Job, of the Old Testament, lost all his children and was stripped of everything he owned; yet, he proclaimed, "Though He slay me, yet will I hope in Him" (Job 13:15a). Job was convinced of the sovereignty of God. Instead of cursing God and dying, as his wife suggested, he "tore his robe and shaved his head. Then he fell to the ground in worship" (Job 1:20). He did not ask "Why me?" He did not say "Poor me." He did say, "Shall we accept good from God, and not trouble?" Job 1:22 says, "In all this, Job did not sin by charging God with wrongdoing." Because God chose to do so, "the LORD made (Job) prosperous again and gave him twice as much as he had before" (Job 42:10). Even before Job had everything restored and while still in poverty and pain, he said, "(N)o plan of yours can be thwarted" (Job 42:2b).

Other verses that speak of God's sovereignty are:

Psalm 115:3   "Our God is in heaven; He does whatever pleases Him."

Isaiah 14:27	"For the Lord Almighty has purposed, and who can thwart Him?"
Isaiah 43:13	"Yes, and from ancient days I am He . . . when I act who can reverse it?"
Isaiah 46:10	"My purpose will stand, and I will do all that I please."
Daniel 4:35b	"He does as He pleases . . . No one can hold back His hand."
Lamentations 3:37	"Who can speak and have it happen if the Lord has not decreed it?"
Ecclesiastes 7:14	"When times are good, be happy; but when times are bad, consider: God has made the one as well as the other."

Why is knowing about and believing in the sovereignty of God important? It is important because sometimes it is the only thing that makes sense. It is the only answer to many of life's problems. It is the only reason for hope. If God did not have a purpose for trials, though we may not be privy to that purpose, the paths taken by those we love would sink us into despair. But He is in control and His purposes are sure. He works out everything in conformity with the purpose of His will (Eph 1:11b).

There are many reasons why God allows trials to come into the life of His children. Romans 8:22 tells us that trials are a part of life because we are living in a fallen world. Death came through sin and was passed on to all men. "Therefore, just as sin entered the world through one man, and death through sin, and in this way death came to all men, because all sinned" (Rom 5:12). But, "For as in Adam all die, so in Christ all will be made alive" (1 Cor 15:22).

There is hope.

Trials can come because others sin. Jonah 1 tells us of the danger and distress those in the ship experienced when Jonah was running from God's direction. Proverbs 10:1 tells us that a wise son (or daughter) brings joy to the father, where a foolish son (or daughter) brings grief to the mother. Sin does not just affect the person who is sinning but all who love her as well.

Often trials are the consequence of our own sin. Galatians 6:7b says, "A man reaps what he sows." David experienced sorrow and grief because of sin. In Psalm 51, he acknowledges that sin and who it was ultimately against. "Against you, you only, have I sinned and done what is evil in your sight" (v. 4). He asked to be cleansed and washed, to have a pure heart created within him, to restore the joy he once had, and for a tongue and lips to praise the Lord. His true repentance caused him to pen, "a broken and contrite heart, O God, you will not despise" (v. 17b).

Sometimes a trial is given so God can expand your usefulness. Sometimes you learn better through trials, and what you learn makes you more usable to God. You minister more effectively when you go through a trial and allow God to comfort you. God knows that to experience pain helps one understand a fellow Christian's pain. Ministering to hurting people is more effective if you can say, "I have been there. I understand." You can only say that if you have had a similar experience.

Second Corinthians 1:4 says that God comforts us " . . . so that we can comfort those in any trouble with the comfort we ourselves have received from God." What better way to minister to someone than when you share his/her situation by experience. As you fully trust God and acknowledge His constant care through His sovereignty, you can testify of His faithfulness. God does comfort His children. Isaiah 49:13b - "For the Lord comforts His people and will have compassion on His afflicted ones." Isaiah 51:12a - "I, even I, am He who comforts you." Isaiah 66:13a - "As a mother comforts her child, so will I comfort you." God comforts the downcast (2 Cor 7:6).

It is easy to get comfortable in your Christian walk and forget the needs of others. If the home is tranquil, finances are stable, everyone is healthy, church is a vital part of life, and there are no major problems, it is often hard to actively get involved with other people's problems. This is how the life of Job reads in the first half of chapter one. "Job . . . was blameless and upright; he feared God and shunned evil. He was the greatest man among all the people of the East" (Job 1:1b, 3b). If Job had not been tested by God, we would not know of his anguish when he said, "Why did I not perish at birth?" (Job 3:11a) or "Why was I not hidden in the ground like a stillborn child?" (Job 3:16a) or "I have no rest, but only turmoil" (Job 3:26b). We would not read, "To God belong wisdom and power; counsel and understanding are His" (Job 12:13) or "I know that my Redeemer lives and…in my flesh I will see God" (Job 19:25a, 26b) or "But He knows the way that I take; when He has tested me, I will come forth as gold" (Job 23:10).

We grow spiritually and learn the most through suffering, trials, and adversities, because obedience is learned by what is suffered. God has a purpose when parents suffer because of the choice their daughter has made to live in sin. God can bring comfort and strength in the hardest of times, but the purpose is not just so you can be comforted and have the strength to honor God, but so that you can be a comforter and point to the greatest of all Comforters. God will enable you, by the things you learn, to come along side other parents and effectively minister to them in their time of need.

Among the marks of the early church was devotion to the apostles' teachings, fellowship, and prayer. Also, "(T)hey gave to anyone as he had need" (Acts 2:45). This, no doubt, had to do with physical possessions and needs, but the principle remains the same. If fellow Christians are in need of encouragement and comfort, and you can help them because of the things you have learned in obedience, you are obliged to do so. Blessings await anyone who gives sacrificially as those in the early church often did. You cannot give what you do not have, but God faithfully equips His children for ministry. Sometimes the equipment comes in the form of trials and heartaches and learning the godly way they are to be handled. Parents must decide what to do when trials come their way; e.g., they can withdraw and continue to ask "Why" and become bitter, they can excuse the sin and act as though it does not exist, they can make excuses, or they can deal with the sin in a Biblical way.

In Isaiah 38:17a, Hezekiah declares, "Surely it was for my benefit that I suffered such anguish." He made this statement after he had won a victory in battle, only to be told to get his house in order because he was going to die. He cried out to the Lord, weeping bitterly, and God answered his plea to spare his life. God gave Hezekiah 15 more years. Did God change His mind? Was Hezekiah's plea so heartrending that God re-considered His original plan? Absolutely not. This was all under the umbrella of God's sovereign will from the beginning of time. For some reason, known only to God, it was for Hezekiah's benefit that he was led down this path.

God's purposes may not always be clearly understood. Very often they make no sense at all, but it is during those times that the Christian, by faith, learns obedience to God's Word and the faithful following of what it says. "Trust in the Lord with all your heart and lean not on your own understanding" (Prov 3:5). Romans 8:28 assures us that God works all things out for the good of those who love Him and have been called according to His purpose. God has an eternal purpose which He will accomplish.

When the pain returns and the desire to see your daughter repent continues to weigh heavy on your heart, you may wonder if the Lord has forgotten you and if He knows the sorrow you are carrying. David had similar thoughts as penned in Psalm 13. We are not told if this Psalm depicted a certain occasion in David's life or if it was, in general, a sad time that he sometimes experienced. David was so depressed that he questioned whether God had forgotten him forever or had just decided to hide His face from him for awhile. He questioned how long he would be at the mercy of his enemy (vv. 1, 2). After he asked these five questions, David appealed to God for answers. He prayed to be kept alive so his enemies would not overcome him and rejoice about it (vv. 3, 4). After his supplication, David's prayer turned to praise and rejoicing. That led him to put his trust in God's unfailing love (v. 5). Immediately, David decided to sing to the Lord exclaiming His goodness.

As the years roll by, parents will struggle with the same questions with which David struggled. They will continue to look to God for answers while trying to live a God-honoring life. Knowing God is in control makes it possible to trust in His unfailing love and actually have joy in the midst of pain.

David came through very trying times when he thought God might not even be around. If He were around, He had hidden and showed no concern for David's sorrowful heart. This is never true of God. Not only is He with you always (Matt 28:20), He promises, "Never will I leave you; never will I forsake you" (Heb 13:5). Isaiah 41:10 tells us not to fear or be dismayed for God will strengthen and help and uphold with His righteous right hand.

You should not be surprised when you find yourself at odds with your daughter who is living in homosexuality. The conflict is a spiritual one, and because you cannot compromise your conviction and as long as she is unwilling to repent, the conflict will continue. If you were willing to deny the basic principles of God's Word, the tensions might ease; but before God, you cannot. Peter speaks to this very issue in 1 Peter 4:12-13, "Dear friends, do not be surprised at the painful trial you are suffering, as though something strange were happening to you. But rejoice that you participate in the suffering of Christ, so that you may be overjoyed when His glory is revealed."

Remember what Paul said to the Christians in Corinth. He told them they may be hard pressed, but they were not crushed; they may be perplexed, but they were not in despair; persecuted, but not abandoned; struck down, but not destroyed (2 Cor 4:7, 8). Because of this promise, you do not have to lose heart (v. 16). There is triumph through pain.

Facing a trial in a God-honoring way can be a learning process that will enable you to look at your walk with the Lord and evaluate your commitment. Do you find it easy to trust God when things are going well but hard to trust Him when they are not? Examining your heart in the light of Scripture may reveal areas that you need to change and priorities that need to be rearranged.

There is a measure of comfort when suffering is viewed as part of God's overall plan for the Christian life. James 1:2-4 says that God's children are to count it joy whenever they face trials, "because you know that the testing of your faith develops perseverance. Perseverance must finish its work so that you may be mature and complete, not lacking anything." "It seems clear then that the foremost reason God tests us through suffering is to test the strength of our faith."[53]

Abraham was tested; Joseph was tested; Daniel and the three Hebrew children were tested. Esther, Hannah, and Paul, along with all those listed in Hebrews 11, were tested, and that testing resulted in a strengthening of their faith. Events, seen as setbacks, often serve to launch the Christian into periods of spiritual growth.

Men and women who are only marginally interested in

growing spiritually will find it hard to deal with suffering. Instead of accepting adversity as part of God's plan for them, they will see it as something done to them. Ephesians 4 says that God's people should grow up in all aspects unto Him so as not to be tossed back and forth and blown around. Deceitful schemes and belief that adversity is not an integral part of God's working in the lives of His people is taught in some churches. The Scriptures do not teach that. In 2 Corinthians 12:10, Paul said he was content and took pleasure in hardships, persecutions, and difficulties. James 1:12 says the person who perseveres under trial is blessed.

Peter says that our suffering grief in all kinds of trials has "come so that your faith—of greater worth than gold, which perishes even though refined by fire—may be proved genuine and may result in praise, glory and honor when Jesus Christ is revealed" (1 Pet 1:7). In the October, 2002, "Our Daily Bread," the story is told about the 1991 October fire in Oakland, California that destroyed 2500 homes. "The Sunday after the disaster, a local minister carried to his pulpit an unbroken vase, which was the only thing recovered from his home. He asked his congregation, 'Do you know why this is still here and my house is gone'? He answered his own question saying, 'Because this had passed through the fire once before.'"[54]

Job declared, "But He knows the way that I take; when he has tested me, I will come forth as gold" (Job 23:10). Through the grace of God, you can endure fiery trials, disappointments, and heartaches, and, though they are painful, your faith will emerge from the flames purer and stronger than ever before.

The goal of all Christians, and that includes parents, is to please God in every way (2 Cor 5:9; Col 1:10). No one pleases God who "wears" sadness, disappointment, and discouragement on her face. We are called to mirror Christ to the world and to live with the hope that no matter what happens, God is in control, and He will get the glory due Him. The process He is putting you through is so that you will be transformed into His likeness (2 Cor 3:18).

The world advances the view that Christians should not make a big deal out of homosexuality because times have changed and cultures are different. "Lighten up; don't be so narrow. Love is the key—just love everybody and everything." Romans 12:2, 3 says, "Do not conform any longer to the pattern of this world, but be transformed by the renewing of your mind. Then you will be able to test and approve what God's will is— His good, pleasing and perfect will."

God put families together, and in His omniscience He saw how each member would live. He also knows the devastation parents now experience, and He is able to sympathize with them (Heb 4:15). He has seen the times when they wanted to give up, when they did not want to pray because they were not sure how, or had said the same things over and over. He knows the amount of tears they have shed. He knows all about them.

But life goes on, and the purposes for which God placed them in this situation are still sure. Though no one knows the future nor down what path they must go, their confidence is not in the future but in the God of the future. Shadrach, Meshach, and Abednego declared to the king that their God was able to deliver them. They even said He would rescue them, but if He did not deliver them, they still would remain true to their convictions.

"For everything that was written in the past was written to teach us, so that through endurance and the encouragement of the Scriptures we might have hope" (Rom 15:4).

See Appendixes H, I, J

CHAPTER X

BIBLICAL COUNSEL FOR DAUGHTERS

✀

"After it became clear to me that what I was experiencing was more than a temporary inclination toward women, I attempted suicide. At thirteen years of age, I saw no way out of a devastating situation. It was apparent to me that God was not going to change me, so I tried to take the matter into my own hands. I swallowed an entire bottle of aspirin."

"I was born a homosexual, which means God made me this way. Since I am made in His image, He is pleased with me. It is His gift to me; therefore, I will celebrate my homosexuality because it is good."

These two quotes are typical examples of those who struggle with homosexuality. They are the opposite extremes, and there are many and varied scenarios between. The first quote is one of desperation and hopelessness because no Biblical direction was found. The second quote shows giving in to homosexuality. She, no doubt, experienced guilt, tried to change, gave up, and to soothe her conscience, bought into lies. Some daughters are tired of struggling and decide to end their lives. Some figure out a way to justify themselves and put up barriers of protection. Is there help for just one kind of struggler or are there answers for both?

Where is the best place to start? How do you reach both the downcast and the arrogant? Should your approach be different? You must begin with the truth about what homosexuality is. Since we find answers to life's most complicated problems in the wisdom of God through His Word, that is where we go for definitions and remedies. Medical science, genetics, philosophy, and psychology do not have the answers, for God has made foolish the wisdom of the world. "For the message of the cross is foolishness to those who are perishing, but to us who are being saved it is the power of God" (1 Cor 1:18). The wisdom of this world does not lead to Christ and when compared to God is foolish. "For the foolishness of God is wiser than man's wisdom, and the weakness of God is stronger than man's strength" (1 Cor 1:25).

Some daughters are not willing to hear the truth. If she displays hostility or refuses to discuss the issues, pray that God will give some windows of opportunity so that from time to time words will be spoken to her that will be used by the Holy Spirit to convict. Pray for this daughter as for anyone who is not serving the Lord.

Since daughters come from various backgrounds and different understandings concerning spiritual things, it will be necessary to learn as much about her as possible. Some have no spiritual training at all, while others have been schooled from a very early age. One may think homosexuality is wrong but has never named it sin. One may know it is sin, has begun to question that fact and given up hope since prayer has not seemed to work. One, after years of tears, struggles, and reverting back, may be trying to convince herself that it is acceptable for some people to live in homosexuality. Another may truly be looking for help and be willing to do whatever it takes.

If a "lesbian" seeks counsel and has no knowledge of Scripture, begin with the simple plan of salvation. Explain to her what it means to be a Christian and invite her to confess her sins in repentance and be forgiven. Disciple her as any new believer. Get her involved in church and encourage strong Christians her age to befriend her. As confidence builds in the relationship and the study of the Bible continues, the Holy Spirit will convict and continue a work of sanctification in her life that will result in her pursuing a life of holiness and obedience to the Lord.

Might she struggle? Yes, she will struggle like anyone who has had a life-dominating sin. She will need help and encouragement to restructure all areas of her life. She needs someone to whom she is accountable on a weekly basis—maybe more often at the beginning. She should be encouraged to stay busy. Someone should be available to her whenever her struggle would seek to overwhelm her. She is a babe in Christ. She is walking down a strange, unknown path, and she will need lots of reassurance. The homosexual community will be available to welcome her back, so Christians must do a better job and be even more available.

For the daughter raised in a home where the Bible was the standard, the question as to whether homosexuality is a sin is no longer an easy question to answer. She always thought it was a sin, but now she wonders. The reason there are questions is probably because she, herself, is struggling with this sin and has cried out to the Lord over the years but is still being tempted in this area.

She will try to explain her homosexual desires as something other than sin. The desire is so strong, it seems different to her than the sin of lying, for example. It seems different than being tempted to steal something or not give back money when given too much change. This struggle is different, she will reason. She does not want to be this way; she does not want to feel this way or have these desires, but she does. She has asked God over and over to take all of this away, but it remains.

This is different, she will rationalize, than jealousy, slander, lying, or anger. These sins are just what people allow themselves to do, she argues. But this attraction for another woman is different, and "Even though I wish I were different, I am not. This is the way I am."

If she continues to reject the truth that homosexuality is a sin, the counterfeit will look real and easier, and she will be deceived. Second Thessalonians 2: 9 ff tells us that deception is "in accordance with the work of Satan" who is out to deceive those who are perishing. "They perish because they refused to love the truth and so be saved. For this reason God sends them a powerful delusion so that they will believe the lie and so that all will be condemned who have not believed the truth but have delighted in wickedness."

Unless she is convinced that the Bible calls homosexuality a sin, she will not have the strength or courage to fight the battle—and it will be a battle. The devil is always persistent in tempting us in our weakest areas. After Jesus had fasted for 40 days, the devil knew He would be most vulnerable in the area of hunger, so he tempted our Lord there first. Jesus used the Word of God to resist him and win the battle.

Again, being convicted in her heart that homosexuality is indeed a sin is just the starting point. Any doubt, or any wavering will impede progress. Looking for any other answers, trying to rationalize (anything other than acknowledging it as sin), and the battle is lost. Anything other than confessing homosexuality as sin and repenting in tears will lead to a hopeless life of bondage and defeat. She must be convinced in her heart.

After she calls sin, sin, she must resist anyone or anything that does not do the same. "Do not give the devil a foothold" (Eph 4:27). There are plenty of voices in the world whose purpose is to cloud the truth of Scripture. John warns about them in 1 John 4: 5, where he says people from the world speak from the viewpoint of the world. Do not listen to the world but listen to those who have heard from God through His word. You can overcome because "the One who is in you is greater than the one who is in the world."

False teaching and views that contradict the message of the Bible come from those who call themselves "gay Christians." It is true that they have a form of religion, but they are not holding to the true teachings of God's Word. The errors are often hard to perceive because they contain some elements of truth, but what they are actually saying is hidden. Paul warns in Galatians 1:9 to be careful. "If anybody is preaching to you a gospel other than what you accepted, let him be eternally condemned." In the verse before that, he said, "But even if we or an angel from heaven should preach a gospel other than the one we preached to you, let him be eternally condemned." In verses 6 and 7, he says this "different gospel" is really no gospel at all. Note carefully that this type of "gospel" is the desertion of the God of grace.

Notice the progression in Galatians 1 of the person who departs from the truth. She deserts Christ Himself (v. 6). When she adds to the gospel, she actually destroys it (v. 7a). She endangers the souls of others, when the gospel is altered (v. 7b). She comes under God's eternal condemnation (v. 8).

Any twisting of the Word of God is the deserting of Christ Himself. Christ and His Word cannot be separated. No one can say "I love God" or "I love Jesus" and not obey His commands. No one can love God and look for ways to do sinful acts. "Whoever claims to live in Him must walk as Jesus did" (1 John 2:6).

The secret lies in this: "Submit yourselves, then, to God. Resist the devil, and he will flee from you. Come near to

God and He will come near to you" (Jas 4:7, 8). The one, though struggling with the sin of homosexuality, must want to please God more than she wants to please herself. She must understand that only as she fully commits her life to Christ will this be possible.

SPECIFICALLY FOR YOU WHO ARE STRUGGLING

First Peter 2:11 warns against sinful desires that war against your soul. If you want to serve God but the temptation to give in to homosexuality seems more than you can bear, the Lord, through the apostle Peter, is speaking to you.

Second Peter 1:3 assures you that God's divine power is all you need for life and godliness, and He will give that power to you. This precious promise is given so that you can participate in the divine nature and escape the corruption in the world caused by evil desires. You are admonished to make every effort to add to your faith moral excellence, knowledge, self-control, perseverance, godliness, kindness, and love. Practicing these will keep you from being ineffective and unproductive. " . . . for as long as you practice these things, you will never stumble" (2 Pet 1:10 NASB). " . . . you will never fail" (NIV).

Following these great words of comfort and inspiration, Peter, in chapter two, warns that there are false prophets and teachers who will secretly introduce destructive heresies, and you must beware of them. These prophets and teachers will follow shameful ways of the world and dispute the truth. God will hold them for the day of judgment. Peter recalls some of God's judgment; e.g., God did not spare the angels when they sinned, but sent them to hell; He destroyed the ancient world, sparing only Noah and his family; God burned Sodom and Gomorrah to ashes because the people lived ungodly and filthy lives. He spared that city's only righteous man, Lot, because God knows how to rescue the godly from temptation (2 Pet 2:4-7). He will do the same for you.

Verse 10 and following describe these false prophets who follow the evil desires of the sinful nature as being bold and arrogant. They are blasphemers, creatures of instinct, and people who cause much harm. They do not exercise reason but judge things according to their senses. They follow the inclinations of their carnal minds. Their vices expose them to the wrath of God and bring them misery and ruin. Yet, they continue to glory in their shame.

Much of what Peter warned about is being displayed in our country today. Several years ago, the city of San Francisco celebrated their sin by sponsoring a Gay Freedom Day Parade. One sign carried in that parade read "GOD IS GAY" (blasphemy). There was a group known as SLUTS (Seminary Lesbians Under Theological Stress). The order of the day was indecent exposure, gyrations, and other immoral acts. With pride, they paraded along—they gloried in their shame. "Their idea of pleasure is to carouse in broad daylight" (2 Pet 2:13b).

"Indecent exposure laws lapse into outmoded times, far too archaic for the enlightened minds of liberal San Francisco. Laws governing public morality are simply suspended for the day in deference to the gay community."[55]

The homosexual community is well organized. Beware. They are out to recruit, confuse, and call into question the teachings of Scripture. To try to weaken family-oriented America, they have designed several strategies. First, there is the strategy to desensitize the public by constantly exposing it to their agenda. More and more exposure produces less and less emotion, and when emotions wane, indifference sets in. Their goal is to "market" homosexuality as legitimate, and call it an alternative lifestyle.

The second strategy is to portray the homosexual as a victim who needs protection, rather than as an aggressive challenger. Third, instead of demanding support for their practice, the homosexuals wants the public to place the emphasis on anti-discrimination so they can be considered a minor group and get certain favors. Fourth, they want to label those opposing homosexuality as homophobics.[56]

Second Thessalonians 2:9-12 says that Satan's work is one of deception, where he deceives those who are perishing. They refuse to love the truth and be saved by it. Because of their refusal to believe the truth, God will send them a powerful delusion and they will believe lies and choose to delight in their wickedness. They will then be eternally condemned.

Beware of those who say you can practice homosexuality and still be a Christian.

Remember, when you depart from Biblical principles, you are departing from Christ because the two cannot be separated. Take careful note of those who say they love Jesus but do not follow His teaching. In Matthew 15:8, Jesus says that there are those who honor Him with their lips but their hearts are far from Him.

Beware of those who talk only about love—love God, love your neighbor, God loves you, love, love, love. "God is love," they quote and then suggest that a loving God would never make people with homosexual desires if He did not want them to act on those desires. Who is hurt, they ask, if two consenting adults are "in love." They totally ignore the holiness of God.

The phrase "God is love" appears only two times in the Bible (1 John 4:8, 16). It is in great error if we take John's "words to be a definitive statement concerning the essential nature of God."[57] If we say literally that God is love, then we must also say that love is God. This would mean we must worship love since love equals God. It would destroy the concept of God's personality and His other attributes. God is also said to be light and truth. "For our soul's sake we must learn to understand the Scriptures. We must escape slavery of words and give loyal adherence to meanings instead."[58]

Beware of those who say little or nothing about the holiness of God. In text after text, God is referred to as the Holy One. "Holy is the way God is. To be holy, He does not conform to a standard. He is that standard. He is absolutely holy with an infinite, incomprehensible fullness of purity that is incapable of being other than it is. Because He is holy, His attributes are holy; that is, whatever we think of as belonging to God must be thought of as holy."[59]

Absolute holiness belongs to God alone. That is why He says "Be ye holy; for I am holy," not "Be ye holy as I am holy."[60] God is calling you to a life of holiness. Hebrews 12:14 tells you to make every effort to be holy because without holiness you will not see the Lord. First, you must put forth effort to be holy and second, you must realize that holiness is a process that lasts a lifetime. The word "'holiness' signifies separation to God and the conduct befitting those so separated. 'Sanctification' is thus the state predetermined by God for believers, into which, in grace, He calls them and in which they begin their Christian course and so pursue it."[61]

"It is God's will that you should be sanctified: that you should avoid sexual immorality; that each of you should learn to control his own body in a way that is holy and honorable, not in passionate lust like the heathen, who do not know God. For God did not call us to be impure, but to live a holy life" (1 Thess 4:3-5, 7). How is this possible?

"Ah, Sovereign LORD, You have made the heavens and the earth by your great power and outstretched arm. Nothing is too hard for you" (Jer 32:17). Matthew, Mark, and Luke record Jesus' words when He declared nothing is impossible with God.

"I can do everything through Him who gives me

strength" (Phil 4:13). These verses are great verses of promise, but how do they play out in the life of someone being tempted everyday with the all-consuming, life-dominating sin of homosexuality?

The testimony of one woman who came out of homosexuality several years ago describes the bondage she experienced. She said she was never satisfied; she felt crushed if her partner did not look at her the right way or did not speak to her in the way she wanted. She looked to her partner for everything—all her "needs." She said these upheavals cannot be compared to a heterosexual relationship because the dependency is "unnatural." It was not a normal relationship where one person depended on another for certain things, but it was an all-consuming losing of yourself in another person. She explained it as total bondage. Quite often her perceived needs were not met, and she became depressed.

Those who have not acted on their homosexual desires in a physical way live in fear because being exposed is their worse nightmare. "What if somebody can tell?" A sense of isolation is also feared—"Is anyone else like me, struggling in this area?"

Whatever the case, God is the answer. God's power can help those who are heavy into homosexuality, those who try to justify every minute, those living in sin and misery, and those struggling to stay out of it. But again, how and where do you begin? What form does this help take? How do you persist, and what will be the outcome? Will it really work? Will it last?

Commitment to obeying God's word because of its truth and sufficiency is where to begin. It is a commitment to live according to its teachings no matter how hard it is.

It was said of the Bereans that they not only received the message but also examined the Scriptures every day (Acts 17:11). It is not enough to just hear the Word of God or even to know it. It takes a total commitment to memorize it or at least be so familiar with it that it is within easy reach all the time. It is what is needed in times when doubt, temptation, and discouragement come. This discipline is as essential as breathing. Knowing God's Word and applying it daily is as vital to spiritual growth and maturity as food is to the body.

You must be fully convinced that God will help to resist temptation and that there simply is no way to compromise your thinking. You can never entertain thoughts of "what if" or "maybe." Paul told Timothy that evil men and impostors are deceived and will deceive others but he (Timothy) was to hold fast, being convinced of what the Holy Spirit says because it would make him wise (2 Tim 3:12-15).

Paul warned Timothy, and it is a warning today, that people will not be interested in sound doctrine, but in doctrine that suits their own desires. They will listen to teachers that say things they want to hear. "They will turn their ears away from the truth and turn aside to myths. But you, keep your head in all situations, endure hardship" (2 Tim 4:4-5).

Hebrews 4:12 says, "For the Word of God is living and active." It is not an out-of-date book with little to say about us in the twenty-first century. "It is very lively and active, in all its efforts, in seizing the conscience of the sinner, in cutting him to the heart, and in comforting him and binding up the wounds of the soul."[62] The Word of God "convinces powerfully, converts powerfully and comforts powerfully."[63] It is so powerful that 2 Corinthians 10:4 says it can pull down strongholds. "Those sinful habits that have become, as it were, natural to the soul, and rooted deeply in it, and become in a manner one with it, are separated and cut off by this sword."[64] Its power to discern will turn the sinner's heart inside out so she will see its vileness and turn to the One who can deliver and sustain her in the hardest of times.

The pull to give in to your sexual desires will be strong.

Voices calling to do the opposite of God's commands will be out there. They will come from the so-called "gay Christians," and they will come from those who say "Let people be who they are." Only the life built on the rock of the Word of God, Christ Himself, will survive when the winds of adversity blow.

In Matthew 7:24-27 and Luke 6:46-49, Jesus tells the parable of two houses and describes the foundations on which each is built. Although this parable has an evangelistic message, as does all of Scripture, Christ's emphasis here was on obedience. He asked those around Him why they called Him "Lord, Lord" but refused to do what He instructed them to do. "It is putting an affront upon him to call him *Lord, Lord*, as if we were wholly at his command, and had devoted ourselves to his service, if we do not make conscience of conforming to his will and serving the interests of his kingdom."[65] It is similar to the mocking of Christ in Matthew 27:29 when He was scorned with "Hail, king of the Jews." Christ simply cannot be separated from His Word. People cannot claim Him as Lord and disobey His commands.

Jesus makes the analogy between the foundation needed to build a secure house and the foundation needed to build one's life so that it can withstand the storms of life. When a woman comes to Jesus, hears His words and acts upon them, or puts what she hears into practice, she then has a strong basis on which to build her life. It is like having a foundation under a house strong enough to withstand the various weather conditions. The life built on Christ is a life that can handle the trials, disappointments and temptations without being blown away or overthrown. A deep commitment to Christ the Rock is the foundation on which this is possible. Vacillating, making excuses, compromising, hesitating—anything short of total surrender and commitment to God— will fail.

The second man Jesus talked about in this parable heard

His words but did not put them into practice. That man's house was built on no foundation at all, so when the torrent struck the house, it immediately collapsed. The sand was washed out from under it, and it tumbled to the ground. Jesus' point was that building your life on anything other than Christ, Himself, will have the same disastrous result. A life apart from the grace of God is a life of disarray, searching, confusion, and eventual ruin.

The steps Jesus outlined are plain. You must first of all come. Second, you must hear what God is saying through His word. Third, you must put into practice what you know to be true. As you daily put into practice the Words of Scripture, you will grow in your faith, and your life will be established on the strong foundation.

To put into practice the words heard means learning what God's commands are and following them. God wants to direct you and all His children's lives through His Word. "Your Word is a lamp to my feet and a light for my path" (Ps 119:105). To live according to God's Word, you must know what it says, what it means, and how it applies to your life.

The Bible is a large book, so to keep you from becoming overwhelmed with its length and depth, it may be beneficial to use two different approaches. One approach is to read it through in its entirety. By reading 15-20 minutes a day, you can read it through in one year. This type of reading will give an overview and reveal its contents. Another approach is a more intensive reading. Limit each reading to a section or a small book at a time and read it slowly, mediating on it verse by verse or section by section.

Knowing God's Word is important because it reveals God to you and helps you to see yourself through God's eyes. It reveals God's mercy and forgiveness. Psalm 130:3,4 says, "If you, O LORD, kept a record of sins, O LORD, who could stand? But with You there is forgiveness; therefore you are feared." Living according to God's Word will keep you from sinning. "I have hidden Your Word in my heart that I might not sin against you" (Ps 119:11). It gives sound counsel (Ps 73:24). Its comfort brings joy (Ps 94:19). It convicts (Rom 7:6). In obeying it, there is great reward (Ps 19:11). The Word of God is foundational.

Obeying God's Word and praying go hand and hand. In Psalm 109:4, David said he was a praying man. "Prayer is the soul's traffic with heaven. God comes down to us by His Spirit, and we go up to Him by prayer."[66] One cannot grow spiritually without prayer. Soon after his conversion, it was said of Paul the Apostle that he began to pray (Acts 9:11). Jesus often withdrew to a solitary place to pray. Prayer is as vital to spiritual growth as food is to physical growth.

The person who practices what is heard is filled with the Spirit. Ephesians 5:18-20 says one is not to be drunk with wine. "Instead be filled with the Spirit." When a person is filled with the Spirit, she will "speak to one another with psalms, hymns and spiritual songs." She will be joyful, and she will be giving thanks to God for everything.

The person who practices what is heard loves others and reaches out to them. She is willing to help a person in need (1 John. 3:17,18). This love is not in word only but also in action. James 2:22 says that faith and actions work together. "Give, and it will be given to you. A good measure, pressed down, shaken together and running over, will be poured into your lap. For with the measure you use, it will be measured to you" (Luke 6:38).

This person will give testimony to God's grace in her life. Jesus says we are to let our light shine (Matt 5:16). Second Timothy 1:8a says, "So do not be ashamed to testify about our Lord." Jesus' last words on earth before His ascension were, "You will be My witnesses . . . to the ends of the earth" (Acts 1:8).

The person with the sure foundation will become a model to all believers (1 Thess 1:7) as she imitates Christ in spite of suffering (1 Thess 1:6). She is able to say along with Paul, "Whatever you have learned or received or heard from me, or seen in me—put it into practice. And the God of peace will be with you" (Phil. 4:9). "Whatever happens, conduct yourselves in a manner worthy of the gospel of Christ" (Phil 1:27a).

This person looks forward with anticipation to the day she will be united with Christ. Paul said he desired to depart and be with Christ, but at that time, it was necessary for him to stay and minister (Phil 1:23,24). "For to me, to live is Christ and to die is gain" (Phil 1:21).

Growing to become the person God wants you to be will take time and effort, and you will not be able to do it alone. You will need to become part of a church where the Bible is central; i.e., a church where the living God is the pillar and foundation of truth (1 Tim 3:15b). God accomplishes his plan for the world through His church. "It is His ordained instrument for calling the lost to Himself and the context in which He sanctifies those who are born into His family. Therefore, God expects (and even demands) a commitment to the church from everyone who claims to know Him."[67]

The spiritual benefits of the local church as you faithfully attend are many. Being part of a local congregation is not an option. The Bible instructs one to not forsake assembling together with other believers (Heb 10:25). The church is the place where believers meet to encourage and admonish one another. It is the place where believers worship the living God together. It is vital to the life of all Christians, therefore, that careful consideration be given when choosing a church.

How can a person discern if a church is true to the Bible and is a place where spiritual growth will occur? What does a church like this do? How would one describe it? The church to which the Christians in Jerusalem went is described in Acts 2:42-47, and that should serve as the criteria. It was a church; i.e., the people, who devoted themselves to the apostles' teaching. That means it taught the "whole counsel of God" (Acts 20:27, NKJV); e.g., it taught the sovereignty, wisdom, and love of God, His grace, power, and justice, His redemption, justification, sanctification, and glorification. It included instructions for all of life (home, marriage, children, school, job, church, and all relationships and problems).

God and His word must be the center of the church because it will help "put into practice what you hear" and what you learn. Programs, clubs, activities, skits, puppet shows - though not wrong in and of themselves—do not build a strong faith, and they lack in their abilities to help believers grow in their faith. Solid, Bible-based, exegetical preaching and teaching is what will strengthen people in their walk with Christ. Paul exhorted Titus that he "must teach what is in accord with sound doctrine" (Titus 2:1)

"All things exist primarily for the glory of God, rather than for our benefit."[68]

After making this statement in his book, Dr. Wayne Mack lists several ways you can tell if a church is man-centered rather than God-centered. A man-centered church will follow extrabiblical traditions to make people feel more comfortable. It will hesitate or avoid dealing with certain doctrines so as not to be offensive. It will choose a worship style based on preference rather than on the Biblical model. It will send people to be counseled by someone outside the church, calling them "experts." The man-centered church will not practice church discipline, necessary for the purity of the church. It will seldom engage in corporate prayer.[69]

When you find a church that teaches the totality of God's word, you will find those within the congregation who will provide you with godly fellowship. The early church ate together in one another's homes. They willingly gave to those in need. They had glad and sincere hearts, praising God together (Acts 2:46,47). The church should be concerned about other people—those within the church and those outside its fellowship. A church following the pattern of Acts will train her people to reach out into the community. It will follow the example of the Macedonian churches in 2 Corinthians 8:1-5 where, "Out of the most severe trial, their overflowing joy and their extreme poverty welled up in rich generosity. Entirely on their own, they urgently pleaded with us for the privilege of sharing in this service to the saints. They gave themselves first to the Lord and then to us in keeping with God's will."

Pray and seek out a godly woman with which to share personal struggles. This should be a woman who is willing to pray for you and with you on a regular basis. Involvement in a weekly Bible study along with diligence in your private time of prayer and Bible study is essential. How vital is prayer in the walk with Christ? In Luke 18:1 Jesus told His disciples to always pray and to not give up. Jesus often prayed; He prayed in public and He prayed in private. He prayed alone and also with His disciples. Paul instructs God's people to "pray without ceasing" (1 Thess 5:17 NASB).

"First and foremost, prayer has been appointed that the Lord God Himself should be honored. In the second place, prayer is appointed by God *for our spiritual blessing,* as a means for *our growth in grace.* Third, prayer is appointed by God for our seeking from Him the things which we are in need of."[70] Prayer is not just about asking God for things; it is much broader. It is communing with Him; it is submitting our wills to Him. The acrostic ACTS may help in the time of prayer. A - adoration, C - confession, T - thanksgiving, S - supplication.

It is so easy to slip into selfish prayers that center around ourselves, our family and friends, our ambitions and desires. Perhaps the disciples experienced something similar to that, for they pleaded, "Lord, teach us to pray" (Luke 11:1). How much more should we pray that prayer. A prayer list may be a helpful tool to broaden the base and assure that the prayer is about far more than personal surroundings and cares.

Along with praying for personal immediate surroundings, and friends and loved ones, consider praying for the pastor and other church leaders, the staff, the Sunday School teachers. Pray for neighbors, the local government officials, judges, police officers, state and local representatives, other churches in the community. Find out the names of some pastors and pray for them by name. Pray for the President of the United States, his cabinet, the vice president, congressmen and congresswomen. Pray for the spread of the gospel locally, statewide, nationwide, and around the world. Pray for the missionaries your church supports and for Christians who are being persecuted in other parts of the world. Pray for the establishment of new churches here and abroad. As the prayer list expands, it will be useful to divide the needs and pray for them several days a week rather than every day.

A life devoted to prayer, humbly acknowledging the need for the Holy Spirit's strength, empowers one to resist the devil and stand firm in the faith (1Pet 5:9). It will help to pray for those who mistreat others (Luke 6:28). Jesus said, "Pray that you will not fall into temptation (Luke 22:40). Prayer is effective even when we cannot express the need in words, for the Spirit helps us by praying for us Himself (Rom 8:26).

As you mature in your walk with the Lord, He will use you in the lives of others. God has given every one of His children spiritual gifts, and He will show you what yours are and how best to use them in His service for His honor and glory. Spiritual gifts are the abilities God gives to those who love Him so they can minister to and edify other people. Some gifts are readily seen because of their nature; others are "behind the scene," so to speak, but all are given and can be used in the Lord's church. This is one of the great blessings of belonging to the Lord and a fellowship of true believers.

Reading the Bible and praying every day, getting involved in a good church, and striving to live as unto the Lord does not mean you will be free from trouble. Jesus said that in this world we will have trouble or tribulations (temptations), but Jesus said to take heart because He has overcome the world. Jesus used the Word of God when He was tempted; Joseph, of the Old Testament, fled when he was tempted. They were both victorious. David did not use the Word of God, nor did he flee. He hung around and investigated; i.e., he asked who Bathsheba was. When he found that she was married, he did not flee, nor did He consider what the Law said. He stepped closer to sin, fell, and suffered grave consequences from that sin.

Since everyone has temptations every day, consider ways to minimize temptations. What are some practical steps necessary, and how can you be sure you are heading in the right direction and making godly decisions?

First, you will need to break off all homosexual relationships—not gradually, but promptly and decisively. As hard as this might be, it is necessary. Since you will no longer have things in common, and a certain comfort zone will be missing, it might not be as hard as you think. You must not be deceived with the idea that you can live a changed life and still have close homosexual friends. Wickedness and righteousness have nothing in common (2 Cor 6:14). You now have a nature that desires spiritual things. Those who are lost have a sinful nature and desire what is contrary to the spirit. Their desires are to gratify that sinful nature; your desires are to live by the Spirit (Gal 5:16-18). You must not entertain the notion that you, in any way, can maintain the friendships you once enjoyed. It is not possible.

Second, some preparation is needed to deal with loneliness. Using the "put off" and "put on" principle of Ephesians

4, you will need to replace the old friendships with people who love the Lord and will help you in your walk with Him. Friendships take awhile to develop so anticipate a period of time when activities will be at a minimum, and have a plan. A prepared list of meaningful "things to do" during this time can be very helpful. It is hard to think of constructive things to do when sadness and loneliness are present.

Loneliness is a universal problem that respects neither gender nor age, but God can use times of loneliness for His glory and as a result grow His children in the faith. It is important to understand that being alone does not always equal loneliness. Being alone can give opportunities to pray and study the Bible without interruptions. It can be a time to draw closer to the Lord, away from activities, and to rely on His power to both comfort and sustain you. Those times will give the opportunity to access life and develop ways to reach out to others. Psalm 68:6 says, "God sets the lonely in families." The church is a family, one body with many members. Do not allow loneliness to throw you into self-pity. Psalm 23:4 says, "Even though I walk through the valley of the shadow of death, I will fear no evil, for you are with me." Second Corinthians 1:3 says, God is "the God of all comfort." Seek out those in the church family with whom to have fellowship.

Third, avoid places that were once visited with regularity. Steer clear of a former "hangout," store, restaurant, or club that hold memories. If some section of the library or a place in the mall stirs temptation, do not go near them.

Avoid situations and things that could lead to temptations; e.g., situations of being alone in close quarters at night, or away from others, with just one other woman. Become involved in group activities. Discard perfume and things of that nature that trigger memories of the past. Discard any music that would be a reminder of a certain person, place, or experience having to do with previous homosexual behavior.

In other words, restructure your life to exclude anything that would hint of the past and cause temptation.

Work hard to replace the things that have been discarded. Throw away cassettes and CDs, and replace them with ones that bring honor to God and ones that help to focus on Christ and new life in Him. Pick a new aroma and begin associating it with the new person. Be surrounded with as many new Christian friends, both male and female, as possible. Do not limit friends to just those who are single, but befriend families and learn from their interactions.

Remember, "Therefore, if anyone is in Christ, he is a new creation; the old has gone, the new has come (2 Cor 5:17). Consider changing your hairstyle, perhaps letting your hair grow. Consider replacing masculine clothing with a more feminine look. The purpose in changing is to represent Christ in the best possible way and to be a testimony of His working in your life.

A change of heart will help you make the necessary changes in life. With the heart change comes new desires that focus on pleasing the Lord. Though this change is definite and immediate, the restructuring of your life will take time. Day by day, as you seek to be more like Christ in dying to self, changes will occur. Do not get discouraged; do not be afraid.

Joshua, an Old Testament man of God, was getting ready to lead the Israelites into a new land—into a new territory. There is much to be learned from his life because of the similarities. This new life in Christ is a new territory, as well. The first chapter of the Book of Joshua includes many encouraging words: "No one will be able to stand up against you . . . I will be with you" (v. 5). "Be strong and very courageous. Be careful to obey" (v. 7). "Do not let this Book of the Law depart from your mouth; meditate on it day and night . . . be careful to do everything written in it" (v. 8). "Do not be terrified; do not be discouraged; for the Lord your God will be with you wherever you go" (v. 9).

"So do not fear, for I am with you; do not be dismayed, for I am your God. I will strengthen you and help you; I will uphold you with my righteous right hand" (Isa 41:10).

See Appendixes E, F, G, K, L, M, N

CHAPTER XI

SUMMARY FOR THE DAUGHTER

∞

Now that you understand the Biblical view concerning homosexuality, only a total commitment to Christ will enable you to live your life in a way that pleases and honors Him. In Galatians 2:20, Paul says, "I have been crucified with Christ and I no longer live, but Christ lives in me. The life I live in the body, I live by faith in the Son of God, who loved me and gave Himself for me." That is total commitment—dying daily to self and living daily for Christ. First Corinthians 6:18-20 says, "Flee from sexual immorality. All other sins a man commits are outside his body, but he who sins sexually sins against his own body. Do you not know that your body is a temple of the Holy Spirit, who is in you, whom you have received from God? You are not your own; you were bought at a price. Therefore honor God with your body."

Purpose in your heart to totally abandon homosexuality and all its facets; strive to remove it completely from your life. In Mark 9:43-47, Jesus said if your hand or foot causes you to sin, cut it off. If your eye causes you to sin, pluck it out. Of course, He was speaking figuratively, but spiritually this is serious and radical amputation. Entertain no thoughts that would in any way compromise your conviction or testimony.

Commit yourself to a life of prayer. Set aside time daily in which you commune with God. Develop a prayer list to include a wide variety of people and places. Ask God to help you get a prayer partner with whom you can pray on a regular basis.

Do not neglect reading God's Word, and find a good plan for its comprehensive study. The Bible will equip you for life, for "All Scripture is God-breathed and is useful for teaching, rebuking, correcting and training in righteousness, so that the man of God may be thoroughly equipped for every good work" (2 Tim 3:16).

Find a church where God's Word is faithfully taught. Enter into its worship and its ministries. Be blessed by its mission and be willing to be a blessing to others as you reach out to them. Reach out to the unsaved, and be a testimony of God's grace in your life.

Be prepared for times of temptation and have a plan when they come. Learn to say "No" to them. "For the grace of God that brings salvation has appeared to all men. It teaches us to say 'No' to ungodliness and worldly passions, and to live self-controlled, upright and godly lives in this present age, while we wait for the blessed hope—the glorious appearing of our great God and Savior, Jesus Christ" (Titus 2:11, 12). A simple test when you are faced with temptation comes in the form of a question; i.e., "Would this please the Lord?" or "Am I thinking more of myself than God in this decision?" Bow in the Lord's presence and ask for His strength to answer these questions honestly. The Holy Spirit will be with you, and He is always willing to help you when you are in need. "The Spirit helps us in our weakness . . . the Spirit Himself intercedes for us" (Rom 8:26).

When you are lonely and wonder if anyone really cares,

meditate on Scriptures that address this issue. Hebrews 13:5b says, "Never will I leave you; never will I forsake you." Psalm 55:22 says, "Cast your cares on the Lord and He will sustain you; He will never let the righteous fall." What encouragement! Psalm 62:2 says, "He alone is my rock and my salvation; He is my fortress, I will never be shaken."

CHAPTER XII

SUMMARY FOR THE PARENTS

∞

Rejection from someone you love is often harder than death. Not only is the rejection a rejection of you and everything you hold dear, it is, more importantly, the rejection of Christ Himself and His wonderful plan of redemption. You will learn, over time, however, that life must go on. Things will stay much the same and, at the same time, be very different.

There are several ways you can live your life. One way is to continue allowing yourself to be consumed with how your daughter is living, where every waking moment is shadowed by her sin. If you do this, you will nurse the hurt and anger until it becomes full-blown bitterness. Bitterness is called a root in the Bible and is very hard to eradicate. It will rob you of your joy and any meaningful living. Do not allow this to happen.

Another way to go on with life is to drift so far from your daughter that there is little or no relationship with her. This perhaps is the easiest way to handle things, especially if your daughter is living elsewhere. Since you will not know about her friends, the places she visits or the activities in which she engages, the reopening of wounds will be at a minimum. Living this way is living to protect yourself. If you allow this to continue, you will lose all opportunities to show her the love you still have for her, and you will have no opportunity to speak to her about repentance and God's forgiveness.

Keeping in touch is important. The contacts do not have to be for long periods of time nor do they have to be often. The important thing is that the contacts be consistent and regular. Praying between and during such visits will help make the time with her profitable and may possibly be used by God to minister to her. Remember, this is another sinful lifestyle or life of sin. Would you abandon her if she were living in an adulterous heterosexual relationship or if she were a convicted felon serving prison time? Also, remember Jesus' words in John 6:44, "No one can come to Me unless the Father who sent me draws him." When you feel helpless, the Holy Spirit is at work.

The best way to live, however, is to be fully committed to God yourself and to keep your focus on Him. Make it a practice to pray daily for your daughter, your spouse, and other family members. Take solace in the fact that God is working out all things for your good and His glory. As tempting as it will be, do not withdraw from people and activities. Making yourself available to friends and acquaintances is the best way to focus your attention away from your heavy heart and onto something that will bring glory to God.

It is during the difficult moments and times of deep distress that you can develop a greater love, appreciation, and commitment to the Lord. It is during these times that you experience His strength and are assured of His understanding. David said, "I will be glad and rejoice in Your love, for You saw my affliction and knew the anguish of my soul" (Ps 31:7). "The Lord preserves the faithful" (Ps 31:23b). Remember, when you do not know what to do, God promises, "I will instruct you and teach you in the way you should go; I will counsel you and watch over you" (Ps 32:8).

When you graciously accept from the sovereign Lord His plan for your life, as hard as it may seem, God will bring people into your life to whom you can minister. If you have experienced difficulties, it is easier for people to accept what you have to say. Second Corinthians 1:3, 4 tells us that God comforts you so that you can comfort others. Again, in 2 Corinthians 1, Paul said he and his companions were under such great pressure that they despaired even of life. You have been there. He continued by saying that in their hearts they felt the sentence of death. Sound familiar? "But, this happened that we might not rely on ourselves but on God . . . on Him we have set our hope" (2 Cor 1:9, 10).

In an agricultural setting where everything depended on crops and animals, Habakkuk said these words, "Though the fig tree does not bud and there are no grapes on the vines, though the olive crop fails and the fields produce no food, though there are no sheep in the pen and no cattle in the stalls, yet I will rejoice in the LORD, I will be joyful in God my Savior" (Hab 3:17,18).

Jesus said, "Heaven and earth will pass away, but my words will never pass away" (Matt 24:35). Herein lies your hope.

VERBATIM COUNSELING — PARENTS

∾

Helpful Model for Counselors

Counselor = Cr Counselee = Ce

This counseling session is the first of several. The verbatim session begins after the counselee (Ce) has been welcomed by the counselor (Cr). The counselor has previously read the Personal Data Inventory (PDI) and has spent a few minutes getting acquainted. The mother and father are both Christians and have raised their children in the church. All their children made a profession of faith in Christ between the ages of 10 and 12. To the question "What is the main problem," found on the PDI, the parents replied that they are heartbroken and are seeking counseling because they found out recently that their 20-year-old daughter, who is a junior in college, is living in the homosexual lifestyle. They want help in "coping" with the changes in their family.

Cr   Tell me how you found out about your daughter.
Ce   A dear friend of ours was brave enough to tell us of some rumors she was hearing.

Cr Did you have any suspicions before your friend talked to you?
Ce Only slight suspicions.
Cr What caused those suspicions?
Ce Only that our daughter dated some fine young men when she was 18 and 19 and then seemed to have no interest in dating.
Cr Anything else?
Ce Yes, the endearing way she talked to a particular girlfriend on the phone sent up red flags, but we dismiss it, thinking we were just overly protective.
Cr How did you find out the truth?
Ce After our friend spoke to us, we asked our daughter.
Cr How? Do you remember what you said?
Ce We said, "Daughter, we have become concerned about you and your walk with the Lord. Could we ask you some questions?
Cr What did she say?
Ce She said, "O.K." We said that we had heard some rumors about her and since rumors can be very damaging and are often not true, we wanted to give her the benefit of the doubt. We said that since she was away at school, we really did not know who her friends were or much about them and that because we love her, what we heard was very disturbing. Right away she appeared to get uncomfortable, and in my heart I knew. She then asked us what we had heard, and we told her that it was reported that she was living as a lesbian. She turned to look out the window and said, "Maybe we had better all sit down." This was unlike anything we had ever experienced. It was like a nightmare.
Cr So, did you sit down?
Ce We did. We sat at the kitchen table, and she began making some shocking statement like "I have never

been attracted to men. I have found a soulmate, and I love her. God made me like I am. My mate and I pray together before we eat, and we believe God is blessing our relationship." And there were more such statements. We were so shocked, we just sat there not knowing what to say. We knew that she knew our thoughts on the matter and what we know the Bible says concerning homosexuality, but we felt we had to say something. When we tried to respond, she informed us that she knew what we were thinking and would say so we did not need to discuss the matter. She got up and said she needed to run some errands before heading back to school. In a flash, she was gone.

Cr What did you do when she left?
Ce We cried; we pounded our fists on the table and walked the floor. We became numb and physically weak.
Cr Tell me about the rest of the day.
Ce After she left for college, we walked around in a fog. We prayed. Oh, did we pray! We tried to function but everything seemed different.
Cr What do you mean, different?
Ce We saw her in a different light. We asked each other and ourselves questions. Who had she become? Who is she? Will this pass? What should we do?
Cr And her departure? How did that go?
Ce Strained. She seemed anxious to leave and, to tell you the truth, we were also anxious for her to leave. We needed time to come to grips with what we had just learned.
Cr How long ago did this happen?
Ce About six months ago—no, five months and two weeks ago, and I can remember the exact time of day, too.

Cr Tell me about the last five and a half months. How often do you talk to your daughter? How often do you see her? What has changed? How are you doing?

Ce We used to talk on the phone three or four times a week. Now it is two or three times a month, if that. She used to come home periodically. We have seen her only twice during this time. When we do see her, she seems like a stranger. We are at each other. She is on one side and we are on the other.

Cr And the two of you—what is going on in your lives?

Ce Well, we do not want to be around other people. We go to church and leave right after it is over. We are miserable. We thought this might just be a phase and that when she realized our objections, she would reconsider, but that has not happened. We do not know where to turn or what to do. We do not want people to know. We have even considered moving where no one will know us. We heard about this Biblical counseling ministry in your church and out of desperation have come for help.

Cr What do you think Biblical counseling is?

Ce We are not sure, but it has to be better than some of the stuff we have been reading. Most of it says homosexuality is genetic and therefore the person cannot change. In fact, some of it made us think that we are the ones who need to change. Our daughter once stated that we may have to have counseling in order to accept her the way God made her. <u>Might</u> God accept homosexuality of some sort? As you can see, we are confused along with being heartbroken. We have lost our way. Can you help someone who is tempted to give up?

Cr I am so happy to say yes, although it is not I but the Lord who can lift your heavy burden and give you direction. I am excited to point you to the God who feels your hurts and has the answers to your most complex situations. Hebrews 2:18 says that Christ is able to help those who are being tempted because He, Himself was tempted. And although He was tempted, He did not sin. In Hebrews 4:15, the writer of Hebrews says He is able to sympathize with our weaknesses, having been tempted in every way, just as you are; yet again, He did not sin.

Ce   Why would this happen to a couple who always wanted to serve the Lord and have their children do the same? Is it something we did, or did not do? Is God punishing us, perhaps?

Cr   I cannot possibly answer all of your questions and perplexities, but I can help you to think Biblically, which will relieve your anxiety and worry. What I am seeing, and believe me, the same thing has happened to others, is that you are focusing so much on the problem that God has become blurred. Your daughter's sin occupies the majority of your thinking. You think and pray for little else. Am I right?

Ce   You are so right! We are guilty of neglecting prayer for our other children, but when you hurt as badly as we do, what is the remedy? We believe the Bible and believe God is our answer, but how does it work?

Cr   In answer to a previous question, I believe a starting point would be your never doubting, for a moment, the authenticity of the Bible. By that, I mean you must believe that what it says about homosexuality is true; it is a sin. You must never entertain any thoughts of it being anything other than that. And that is very comforting because the cure for sin is the blood of Christ. You must put to rest any thoughts of what you could have done differently, how it happened, and other questions that probably have no

	answers. You must commit yourselves to prayer, not only for this daughter but for all your children and way beyond the family. You must begin to see the situation through God working in your lives. Instead of your problem being bigger than God, see God as bigger than your problem. Focus on Him and what He can accomplish in your life for His glory.
Ce	How do you do this, practically?
Cr	You do it by retraining your thinking. When your mind begins to dwell on your daughter, and questions like, what if, if only, could it be that...come to mind, begin to think of things that are true, noble, right, pure, lovely, admirable and excellent, as we are encouraged to do in Philippians 4:8. Much of your battle is in your mind.
Ce	That is not easy, because I spend a lot of time trying to figure it all out.
Cr	When the Bible says that God works out all things for the good of those who love Him and have been called according to His purpose, what does that mean? Does that apply to you in this situation?
Ce	It has to, I suppose, because we do love the Lord but I cannot see any good that we will gain because our daughter lives in sin.
Cr	The verse following Romans 8:28 says that God has predestined us to be conformed to the likeness of His son. How do you see that applying to you and your family, and does it make it easier to understand the first verse?
Ce	I guess we become more like Christ when we suffer. Is that what that means?
Cr	Romans 12:2 says, "Do not conform any longer to the pattern of this world, but be transformed by the renewing of your mind. Then you will be able to test and approve what God's will is—His good, pleasing

	and perfect will."
Ce	I did not realize there were so many verses about thinking and your mind in the Bible. What if things become so bad you cannot handle it? People have had breakdowns over similar things. We have almost been to that point. In fact, we have thought of asking our doctor for medication to help us, at least for a while.
Cr	I can assure you that as you trust God daily, you will not become overwhelmed with this problem. Let us look at two verses which I am asking you to begin memorizing. The first answers your question about not being able to handle the stress. First Corinthians 10:13 says, "No temptation has seized you except what is common to man. And God is faithful; He will not let you be tempted beyond what you can bear. But when you are tempted, He will also provide a way out so that you can stand up under it." What is this saying? What promise do you see?
Ce	I think it is saying that God will not put more on us then we can carry. Is that right?
Cr	It is, and what else?
Ce	It is saying that we will be tempted, but we will be able to stand and not fall.
Cr	Before you ask how, let us look at another verse. Second Peter 1:3 tells us, "His divine power has given us everything we need for life and godliness through our knowledge of Him who called us by His own glory and goodness." What does this verse mean?
Ce	It says that God's power is all we need.
Cr	And how does one get that divine power?
Ce	Through knowing about God.
Cr	It is more than knowing about God. It is knowing Him and learning about how He works, seeing Him through the revelation He gives us in the Bible. It

comes through the careful study of His Word, through prayer, and through the fellowship of believers. It comes through seeing God work in the hearts and lives of those to whom we reach out in ministry. It is very easy to be consumed with ourselves when we face the kind of heartache you are facing, but God would have you rest in His promises, pick up your responsibilities, and start living in a way that will bring honor and glory to His name. Often we think our problem is so horrendous that no one could possibly hurt as badly as we are hurting. But if you remember in 1 Corinthians 10:13, there is a phrase that says temptation is common to man. Do you remember that? So, even though people's problems are different, they are the same in many ways. Let us not skip over another phrase in that verse, "God is faithful."

Ce I am sure we have read that verse before, but now it really makes sense to me.

Cr I have a booklet called "Christ And Your Problems" written by Jay Adams. In this book, he expands on 1 Corinthians 10:13. I want you to read that booklet this week and do the questions that go with it. Can you do that?

Ce We certainly will try.

Cr When you come back next week, we will discuss this verse in more detail to see how it applies to your specific problem. We will also go over this booklet and the answers to the questions. Before we close in prayer, what questions might you have?

VERBATIM COUNSELING — DAUGHTER

Helpful Model for Counselors

Counselor = Cr   Counselee = Ce

The counselee is a 23-year-old college student. She was raised by Christian parents in a Bible-believing church. In her second year of college, a friend with whom she eventually shared an apartment, helped lead her into homosexuality. Both girls, claiming to be Christians, knew their relationship had gone beyond just friendship. They knew they were sinning. They tried to end it, but since they continued to live together, they found that next to impossible. They both sought Christian counseling at the beginning, but nothing seemed to work.

The first session of counseling was one of data gathering—both core and halo. At times, the counselee seemed unsure and vulnerable; at other times, she seemed determined to stay in the homosexual lifestyle, while claiming to serve the Lord. The fact that she had come indicated doubts. The counselor questioned her about her relationship with Christ, and she said she was a Christian and loved the Lord very much. The counselor and she discussed some Biblical principles for relationships, and she revealed certain things. One thing was that early in life, she had been more attracted to girls than guys. She was battling why she had those feelings while other girls did not.

She left the first counseling session still wanting to believe that in some cases, homosexuality was not a sin. If one is born that way, she had said, how can it possibly be wrong. Her homework assignment was to read and study passages of Scripture about relationships that God blesses. She was also given several verses about homosexuality and was asked to find in them any possibility of God's blessing.

Cr   For homework, I assigned you some Bible verses about relationships that are blessed by God. Tell me about Genesis 2:20b-25. What relationship did God establish in the beginning? Whose idea was marriage?

Ce   Well, that is the story of Adam and Eve, and they were the first husband and wife. I guess God decided to create or invent marriage. I never really thought much about that.

Cr   Correct; so, what do you think about the relationship between a husband and a wife?

Ce   What do you mean?

Cr   Is it a relationship that would be blessed by God? Is it something with which He would be pleased?

Ce   Yes, of course. But what does this have to do with me. I do not plan to marry.

Cr   Perhaps not, but I want you to see what God's design for relationships were from the very beginning. We will get to more specifics later. OK?

Ce   I guess so, but I still do not see the relevance.

Cr   Let us look at our next verse. What did you learn from Malachi 2:13-16?

Ce   That God hates divorce.

Cr	Yes, and what about Matthew 19:4-6; what did Jesus say about marriage?
Ce	He said to leave your father and mother, and something about divorce and adultery.
Cr	You are correct. Now look back at the very beginning of verse 4. From what is Jesus quoting?
Ce	I do not know.
Cr	Jesus is quoting from Genesis. Remember what we talked about when we read Genesis 2 together? Jesus is affirming the fact that He made humans the same, but also very different—male and female. He said they shall be united in marriage and become one flesh. Mark 10 also records Jesus' word on a husband and wife relationship. Mark further states that what God has joined together no one should separate.
Ce	I am glad you mentioned Jesus, because you know, He never condemned lesbianism. In fact, Jesus never mentioned homosexuality at all. Do you not think that tell us something?
Cr	What do you think that fact tells us?
Ce	I think since Jesus did not condemn it, no one else should. I believe people are born homosexual. Oh, I also think that some are drawn into it because of events in their lives, but mostly I believe God made some people that way. I have friends who would attest to that. In fact, I think that is the way I am. I never wanted these feelings. In fact, you have no idea how much I have prayed about how I am.
Cr	There are many avenues that we could discuss at this point, but let us look at this one which you just now mentioned, namely, what Jesus might have thought about homosexuality. First of all, would you agree from reading the verses we just looked at and others that were assigned, that marriage was God's idea and a relationship He would have us pursue?

Ce	For most people, I guess, but not for all. What if a person has no desire for marriage? What about that?
Cr	Actually, the Bible says that if you do not have the desire to marry, you should not. By being single, you can concentrate on serving God and not have to divide your time with a spouse and children. But that is not what you are talking about, is it?
Ce	No, I mean what if you want a relationship like a marriage but with another woman? What if God puts a desire in a woman for another woman?
Cr	First of all, I do not believe God puts the desire to sin in anyone. Second, do you think Jesus would approve of something the Scriptures condemn in every form?
Ce	What do you mean?
Cr	The Bible calls homosexuality an abomination; it says it is detestable. Are you familiar with that verse in Leviticus 20:13?
Ce	Yes, but that does not apply to us today. It is talking about prostitution and, of course, that is wrong.
Cr	On what do you base your last statement?
Ce	Oh, I read and talk to people, and that is what everyone is saying.
Cr	Let me see if I understand what you are saying. Are you saying that homosexuality is wrong only if it is linked to prostitution? In other words, if it just involves two people, God would approve?
Ce	Yes. Basically, I seriously doubt that if two people love each other and just stay with each other that anything could be wrong.
Cr	I can see that you have a lot of questions and that you have been looking for answers. I trust that you are now seeking answers that are Biblically-based. Otherwise, you would not be here for Biblical counseling. Am I correct?

Ce	I am not sure what I want. At times, I think what I am doing is wrong; at other times and around my friends, I think something different. I guess I am confused.
Cr	The fact that you have come seeking is encouragement to me and it lets me know that I can help you by directing you to the Bible. I cannot, however, help you to justify living in homosexuality. I can help you see the clear teachings of Scripture, and I can pray that the Holy Spirit will guide you into all truth. How willing are you to search the Bible with me and call upon God to show you His truth? How willing are you to change?
Ce	I am willing to give it a try. How long will it take? What do I have to do? How hard will it be?
Cr	Those are all good questions and you will have answers to all of them as our sessions progress. First of all, though, I do not think you can get very far until you agree with the Scriptures that homosexuality is a sin. If you entertain any thoughts that it is other than sin, our whole premise is lost. Can you do that?
Ce	I can try. Can you convince me?
Cr	I do not want to convince you; I want the Holy Spirit, through God's Word, to do that.
Ce	That is kind of what I meant.
Cr	Please turn to Romans 1 and read verses 22 through 26.
Ce	(Ce reads this passage)
Cr	Because these people did not honor God, this passage says God gave them over to sinful desires of the flesh. The sinful desires of the flesh manifested themselves is what manner? Look at verse 26.
Ce	It says that the women exchanged natural relations for unnatural ones. Is that what you mean?

Cr	Yes; what do you think that means?
Ce	I guess it means they slept together like a husband and wife.
Cr	Yes; and what was God's response when they did not consider the knowledge of God to be worthwhile? Read verse 28.
Ce	They did what they should not have done.
Cr	And what does verse 32 say they deserve?
Ce	It says that those who do such things deserve death.
Cr	How serious does this passage of Scripture take homosexuality?
Ce	Very seriously.
Cr	What do you think God calls homosexuality?
Ce	A sin; but again, could this not be connected to prostitution?
Cr	This says nothing about prostitution, but if it did, can you see any room for God's acceptance of same-sex relationships?
Ce	Not really.
Cr	In case you still have some doubt, let us look at 1 Corinthians 6:9-11. This clearly-stated passage says that the wicked will not inherit the kingdom of God, and then it lists who the wicked are or what they do. Among that list are the sexually immoral, idolaters, adulterers, male prostitutes and homosexual offenders.
Ce	Are you saying that homosexuals will not go to heaven?
Cr	I am not saying that; I am showing you what the Bible says. But there is great hope. Verse 11 says that if you are washed in the blood of Christ and grow in your walk with Christ, which is called sanctification, you will be justified. The people Paul is writing to used to live in these types of sin, but because of Christ, they are now living a life that is

	pleasing to God.
Ce	I see.
Cr	Do you also see that because homosexuality is a sin, it has a remedy? Do you see that thinking it is a disorder or is genetic, produces little to no hope?
Ce	I do. If homosexuality is a sin, then the cure is Christ, right?
Cr	Right.
Ce	Are there other verses that talk about homosexuality?
Cr	Second Peter 2:6-10, talks about the ungodly in Sodom and Gomorrah and their destruction. Jude 7 also speaks about the immorality and perversion that went on in Sodom and Gomorrah.
Ce	You have given me a lot to think about. I am not totally convinced though, especially when I think about my many friends and what they will think and what might happen in the future.
Cr	I am sure you have many fears and questions, but in the light of eternity, what kind of choice do you have? Plus, as you turn your life over to Christ and repent of your sin, He will enable you to live for Him.
Ce	But what if it is too hard? What if I cannot follow through?
Cr	If you are serious about serving the Lord, He will meet every one of your needs. In 1 Corinthians 10:13, God has promised not to put any more on us than we can bear. It says that He is faithful. He would never ask you to do something that you are incapable of doing. Do you believe that?
Ce	In theory, yes; but I know what struggling means, and I usually fail eventually.
Cr	Have you ever truly committed your life to Christ, read the Bible faithfully, prayed daily, and had fellowship with His people in a church that preaches

	the gospel every week?
Ce	No; I cannot say I was ever that serious, although I have tried.
Cr	I believe you want to try, and I know that you are scared. I also know that God will help you. I want to give you a booklet to read this week. It is called *Christ And Your Problem*. There are questions that go with it. Complete them and come next time ready to discuss them. You have a lot of work to do, but believe me, with God's help you will overcome this sin and temptation in your life. Before we pray, do you have any other questions?

APPENDIX

APPENDIX A

BROKENHEARTED

∞

The Bible speaks to the brokenhearted and others in despair. How do the following verses both comfort and give Biblical directions?

Psalm 34:18
___

Psalm 147:3
___

Isaiah 61:1-3
___

II Corinthians 4:8
___

Romans 8:26,27
___

Romans 8:31-34
___

Romans 8:35-39

Job 1:20 - When nearly everything was stripped away from Job, note the three ways he responded.
1. _____ 2. _____
3. _____

Write down your thoughts concerning Job's third response.
_____
_____

Genesis 50:20 - Joseph was rejected, lied about, and forgotten. He remained faithful to God and responded Biblically. Write out Genesis 50:20. _____
_____
_____
_____
_____

In light of Romans 8:28,29 how might you begin to understand your circumstances? _____
_____
_____
_____
_____

APPENDIX B

ROMANS ON HOMOSEXUALITY

∞

Read Romans 1:18-32 and answer the following questions:

1. In verse 18, why did God pour out His wrath against the ungodly and the wicked? _____
   _____
   _____

2. In verses 19, 20 how do you know the wicked were not just confused? _____
   _____

3. Verse 24 says "God gave them over . . . for the degrading of their bodies with one another." Why? (vv. 21-23).
   _____
   _____

4. What other sins are listed in verse 25?
   _____
   _____

5. What happened as a result of those sins listed in "4"? (vv. 26, 27). _____
_____

6. What else did God do? (v. 28). _____
_____

7. What do verses 29 and 31 say happened to them?
_____
_____

8. Why are they without excuse? _____
_____
_____

APPENDIX - B
ANSWERS

Read Romans 1:18-32 and answer the following questions:

1. In verse 18, why did God pour out His wrath against the ungodly and the wicked?
   They suppressed the truth by their wickedness.

2. In verses 19, 20 how do you know the wicked were not just confused?
   God made it plain to them, giving them no excuse.

3. Verse 24 says "God gave them over . . . for the degrading of their bodies with one another." Why? (vv. 21-23).
   They refused to glorify Him; they gave Him no thanks; their thoughts were futile, and their hearts were darkened. They became fools.

4. What other sins are listed in verse 25?
   They exchanged the truth of God for a lie and worshipped and served created things rather than the Creator.

5. What happened as a result of those sins listed in question "4"? (vv. 26, 27).
   God gave them over to shameful lusts—homosexual acts between the women and homosexual acts between men. They were indecent acts.

6. What else did God do? (v. 28).
   God gave them over to a depraved mind.

7. What do verses 29 and 31 say happened to them?
   They became filled with wickedness, evil, greed, depravity, envy, murder, strife, deceit, malice, gossip, slander,

hatred toward God, insolence, arrogance, boastful and more.

8. Why are they without excuse?
   They knew what they were doing deserved death; yet they continued doing them and approved of those who practiced the same.

APPENDIX C

HOPE

∞

After acknowledging that homosexuality is a sin, how is Jeremiah 32:17 an encouragement? _____

1. Read and begin memorizing 1 Corinthians 10:13 and answer the following:
   a. How are Christians assured that their problems are not unusual? _____

   b. How will knowing that others face similar trials be helpful? _____

   c. In what ways are the words "God is faithful" comforting? _____

    d. What promise comes after "God is faithful" in this verse? _____
_____
_____

    e. What promise does this verse give for when you are tempted? _____
_____
_____

2. Read 1 Corinthians 6:9, 10 and list those who will not inherit the kingdom of God. _____
_____
_____

3. How do you know there is hope for any or all of those listed? _____
_____
_____

4. What does this verse say caused them to change?
_____
_____
_____

APPENDIX C
ANSWERS

After acknowledging that homosexuality is a sin, how is Jeremiah 32:17 an encouragement? *God is all powerful and nothing is too hard for Him. He will help in my battle with homosexuality. He forgives, and He will give me the strength I need.*

1. Read and begin memorizing 1 Corinthians 10:13 and answer the following:
    a. How are Christians assured that their problems are not unusual?
    Temptation is common to man—different, no doubt, but much the same.

    b. How will knowing that others face similar trials be helpful?
    Knowing that they have faced trials and have overcome them gives me hope.

    c. In what ways are the words "God is faithful" comforting?
    He will be with me through anything. He will not forsake me. He will give me the power to obey.

    d. What promise comes after "God is faithful" in this verse?
    He will not let me be tempted beyond what I can bear.

    e. What promise does this verse give for when you are tempted?
    He will provide a way out so that I can stand up under the trial.

2. Read 1 Corinthians 6:9, 10 and list those who will not inherit the kingdom of God.
   The sexually immoral, idolaters, adulterers, prostitutes, homosexual offenders, thieves, the greedy, drunkards, slanderers, swindlers.

3. How do you know there is hope for any or all of those listed?
   Verse 11 says that some of them were these, so named, but they were washed, sanctified and justified.

4. What does this verse say caused them to change?
   They were washed, sanctified and justified in the name of the Lord Jesus Christ and by the Spirit of God.

APPENDIX D

A STUDY IN GALATIANS

1. Read and study Galatians 5:16-26 carefully.

2. Who does the one living contrary to the Spirit want to please?_____

3. How does she do this? _____
   _____
   _____

4. How does the one living by the Spirit want to please?
   _____
   _____

5. How does she do this? _____
   _____
   _____

6. List the acts of a sinful nature. _____
   _____
   _____

7. List the fruit that is evident in those being led by the Spirit. _____

8. What does verse 24 tell you those belonging to Christ Jesus have done? _____

9. What does that mean in your life in practical ways?

APPENDIX D
ANSWERS

1. Read and study Galatians 5:16-26 carefully.

2. Who does the one living contrary to the Spirit want to please?
   Herself

3. How does she do this?
   Disregards the Bible's teachings and lives as unto herself.

4. Who does the one living by the Spirit want to please?
   The Lord

5. How does she do this?
   Find out what pleases the Lord and do them.

6. List the acts of a sinful nature.
   Sexual immorality, impurity and debauchery; idolatry and witchcraft; hatred, discord, jealousy, fits of rage, selfish ambition, dissensions, factions and envy; drunkenness, orgies and the like.

7. List the fruit that is evident in those being led by the Spirit.
   Love, joy, peace, patience, kindness, goodness faithfulness, gentleness, and self-control.

8. What does verse 24 tell you those belonging to Christ Jesus have done?
   They have crucified the sinful nature with its passions and desires.

9. What does that mean in your life in practical ways?

APPENDIX E

LONELINESS

A. Sin severs a proper relationship with God. Loneliness is often the result of that broken fellowship. Study and note the effect sin has on a person's relationship with God.
  1. Deuteronomy 32:19-20:

  2. Psalm 66:18:

  3. Proverbs 15:29:

  4. Isaiah 59:2:

  5. Ephesians 2:12:

6. Ephesians 4:17-19:

7. Titus 3:3:

B. What specifically in your life may have contributed to you loneliness?

C. How would God want you to resolve these things? (Use Scriptures)

APPENDIX F

LONELINESS

∞

A. Study these verses and note the ways in which God restores a person to Himself.

1. Colossians 1:20, 22: _____

2. 1 Peter 3:18: _____

3. Romans 3:24: _____

4. Ephesians 1:7: _____

5. Ephesians 2:13-16 _____

6. Hebrews 9:26-28: _____

7. Romans 5:1: _____

B. What hope do you see from these verses that can be applied to your situation? _____
_____

APPENDIX G

LONELINESS

∞

A. Study and note the special promises God faithfully gives to His children in any circumstance.

1. Joshua 1:9: _____

2. Psalm 27:10: _____

3. Isaiah 49:15: _____

4. Psalm 139:6-12: _____

5. Philippians 4:19: _____

6. Matthew 28:20: _____

7. Romans 8:38,39:

B. When or in what circumstances, specifically, do you feel lonely?

C. What are some things the Lord will help you do when you feel yourself heading in that direction?

APPENDIX H

DEPRESSION

A. Study these verses, noting the causes that contribute to depression.

1. Psalm 32:3,4:

2. Psalm 73:1-14:

3. Genesis 4:6,7:

4. Deuteronomy 1:28,29:

5. Psalm 55:2-8:

6. Luke 24:17-21:

7. 2 Samuel 18:33: _____

8. 1 Samuel 1:7,8: _____

9. Habakkuk 1:1-4: _____

B. After studying these verses carefully, to what do you attribute your depression? _____
_____
_____

C. Philippians 4:4 says to "rejoice in the Lord." What does "in the Lord" suggest when a person is dealing with depression? _____
_____
_____

D. List some reasons you have to "rejoice in the Lord."
_____
_____
_____

APPENDIX I

DEPRESSION

∞

Study these verses and note what you must do to overcome depression.

1. Psalm 32:1-6:

2. Psalm 1:1-6:

3. Psalm 40:1-4:

4. Psalm 41:1-3:

5. Psalm 84:4-12:

6. Psalm 106:3:

7. Luke 11:28:

8. John 13:17:

9. James 1:12, 21-25:

10. Philippians 4:1,4:

11. 1 Samuel 2:1-10:

12. Philippians 4:12,18:

13. 1 Corinthians 9:24-27:

14. 2 Timothy 2:5:

15. 1 Thessalonians 5:16-22:

APPENDIX J

OVERCOMING DEPRESSION

∽

Have a plan when you feel depression "approaching" or during those times when it "hits" you without much warning. Have the list within easy reach.

1. Things you can do.
2. Things you need to do.
3. Blessings for which you can thank the Lord.
4. People in need:
   a. What you might do for them.
   b. How you can pray for them.
5. Bake or make something for someone.
6. Write someone a note.
7. Check on the elderly.
8. Have a prayer list and focus on others.
9. Take someone out for lunch or have him/her in your home.
10. Take a walk and enjoy God's nature.

The object of this list is to take the focus off oneself and to begin focusing on others and on the Lord. The worst thing is to sit around or lie around. Practice putting others first, even in your mind.

APPENDIX K

PRACTICAL APPLICATION

∞

1. Read and study Ephesians 4:22-24 and answer the following:
   a. What is Paul saying? _____
   _____

   b. What does this passage mean to you? _____
   _____
   _____

   c. How might you apply it to your life? _____
   _____
   _____

2. Using the "put off" and "put on" principle found in this passage, make a list of things you must put off and a list of things with which you will replace them.

PUT OFF	PUT ON
_____	_____
_____	_____
_____	_____
_____	_____
_____	_____
_____	_____
_____	_____
_____	_____
_____	_____

APPENDIX K
ANSWERS

1. Read and study Ephesians 4:22-24 and answer the following:

   a. What is Paul saying?
   Your former way of life needs to be put off because it is corrupt and a new way of life needs to be put on. Replace the old with the new.

   b. What does this passage mean to you? _____

   c. How might you apply it to your life? _____

2. Using the "put off" and "put on" principle found in this passage, make a list of things you must put off and a list of things with which you will replace them.

PUT OFF	PUT ON

APPENDIX L

PRACTICAL CHANGES

∞

What specific plans have you made in regard to your former way of life, namely:

PLACES

_____
_____
_____
_____
_____
_____

PEOPLE

_____
_____
_____
_____
_____
_____

THINGS

HABITS

APPENDIX M

LIFE-DOMINATING SIN

∞

If a person can be called by the sin he/she commits, it is considered a life-dominating sin; e.g., homosexual, drunkard, thief. These sins affect most areas of that person's life, including eating and sleeping habits, job, emotions, health, and family life.

Study and list how to overcome whatever sin is dominating you.

1. 1 Corinthians 6:9,10: _____

2. Galatians 5:19-21: _____
   _____

3. 1 John 2:16,17: _____

4. Romans 6:14:

5. Ephesians 5:18:

6. Ephesians 4:22-24:

List some examples of this principle:

a. Ephesians 4:25: Example: *put off lying and speak truthfully*

b. Ephesians 4:28:

c. Ephesians 4:29:

d. Ephesians 4:31,32:

Make a list of things in your life that must be put off. Opposite that list, list things that can replace them so that you can glorify God with you life.

APPENDIX N

LIFE-DOMINATING SIN

Specific Plan

First Timothy 4:7 says you are to discipline yourself to be godly. Discipline takes a plan if it is to work. Below are some suggestions for establishing a plan for change.

1. Establish a regular time for Bible reading and prayer.
2. Work every day to memorize key verses; e.g., 2 Peter 1:3 and 1 Corinthians 10:13.
3. Put verses on the bathroom or bedroom mirrors, around the kitchen sink, or on the computer.
4. Let nothing minor keep you from regular church attendance.
5. Keep a journal of the times you are tempted:
   a. What the temptation was
   b. Where you were
   c. Who you were with
   d. What you were thinking about
6. Devise a plan whenever temptation comes and immediately put it into practice.
7. Confide in someone who will pray regularly for you and with you.

ENDNOTES

1. The NIV *(NEW INTERNATIONAL VERSION)* is used throughout this paper except where otherwise indicated. NASB will indicate *NEW AMERICAN STANDARD BIBLE.* NKJV will indicate *NEW KING JAMES VERSION.*
2. Anita Worthem and Bob Davies, *Someone I Love is Gay,* (Downers Grove: InterVarsity Press) p. 114.
3. Chuck & Donna McIlhenny with Frank York, *When the Wicked Seize the City,* (Layfayette, Louisiana: Huntington House Publishers, 1993), p. 17.
4. Worthem, *Someone I Love is Gay,* p. 82.
5. Charles W. Keysor, *What You Should Know About Homosexuality,* (Grand Rapids: Zondervan, 1979 41.
6. Ibid., p. 187.
7. McIlhenny, *When the Wicked Seize a City,* p. 90.
8. Greg L. Bahnsem, *Homosexuality, A Biblical View* (Grand Rapids: Baker Book House, 1978) p. 35, 36.
9. John W. Howe, *Should We Change the Rules?* (Lake Mary: Creation House, 1991) p.12.
10. Matthew Henry's Commentary on the Whole Bible, vol. 6, (N.p., third printing, USA: Hendrickson Publishers, Inc., 1994), p. 300.
11. Ibid.

[12] John Murray, *The Epistle of the Romans,* vol. 1 (N.p., Reprint, Grand Rapids: Wm. B. Eerdmans Publishing Co., 1967), p. 47.
[13] Greg L. Bahnem, p. 59.
[14] John Ankerburg and John Weldon, *The Facts on Homosexuality,* (Eugene, OR: Harvest House Publishers, 1994), p. 39.
[15] Matthew Henry vol. 6, p. 430.
[16] Jay E. Adams, *The Christian Counselor's Commentary, I & II Corinthians,* (Hockettstown, N. J.: Timeless Texts, 1994), p.42.
[17] James B. DeYoung, *Homosexuality* (Grand Rapids: Kregel Publications, 2000), p. 202.
[18] Matthew Henry, vol. 6, p. 895.
[19] *NEW GENEVA STUDY BIBLE* (Nashville, Atlanta, London, Vancouver: Thomas Newlson Publishers, 1995), p. 2000 footnote.
[20] Matthew Henry, vol. 6, p. 896.
[21] Ibid.
[22] John Ankerburg and John Weldon, p.1.
[23] Joe Dallas, *A Strong Delusion,* (Eugene: Harvest House Publishers, 1996), p. 226.
[24] Edward T. Welch, *Homosexuality, Speaking the Truth in Love*, (Phillipsburg: P & R Publishing, 2000), p.2.
[25] Ibid., p. 29.
[26] Ibid., p.4.
[27] Charles W. Keysor, p. 82.
[28] James B. DeYoung, p. 218.
[29] Charles W. Keysor, p. 71-73.
[30] John Ankerburg and John Weldon, p. 36.
[31] James B. DeYoung, p. 60.
[32] Charles W. Keysor, p. 59.
[33] Ibid.
[34] Welch, p. 12.
[35] Ibid.

36 Ibid.
37 Greg L. Bahnem, p. 56, 57.
38 Joe Dallas, p. 110.
39 John Ankerburg and John Weldon, p. 13.
40 Greg L. Bahnem, p. 50
41 James B. DeYoung, p. 156.
42 Edward T. Welch, p. 33.
43 Greg L. Bahnem, p. 60, 61.
44 Anita Worthem and Bob Davies, pp. 63.
45 Sylvia Gunter, *For the Family* (Birmingham: The Father's Business, 1994), p. 18.
46 A. W. Pink, *The Sovereignty of God* (Carlisle: The Banner of Truth Trust, Reprinted 1980), p. 114.
47 Ibid., p. 118.
48 Thomas Watson, *The Godly Man's Picture* (Great Britain: MPG Books Ltd, 1666. Reprinted, Carlisle: The Banner of Truth Trust, 1999), p. 156.
49 Matthew Henry, vol. 6, p. 578.
50 Ibid., p. 579.
51 A. W. Pink, p. 22.
52 Jerry Bridges, *Trusting God* (Colorado Springs: NavPress, 1988), p. 42.
53 John MacArthur, Jr. *The Power of Suffering* (Wheaton: Victor Books, 1995), p. 26.
54 Vernon Grounds, "Tested By Fire," *Our Daily Bread,* (October 25, 2002).
55 Chuck & Donna McIlhenny, p. 15.
56 Ibid., p. 17, 18.
57 A. W. Tozer, *The Knowledge of the Holy* (HarperCollins Publishers: Harper, San Francisco, 1961), p. 97.
58 Ibid., p. 98.
59 Ibid., p. 105, 106.
60 Ibid., p. 106.
61 W. E. Vine, *Complete Expository Dictionary of Old and New Testament Words.* Nashville, Atlanta, London,

Vancouver: Thomas Nelson Publishers. 1984, 1996) p. 307.
[62] Matthew Henry, p. 730.
[63] Ibid.
[64] Ibid.
[65] Matthew Henry, vol. 5, p. 521.
[66] Thomas Watson, p. 87.
[67] Wayne Mack, *Life in the Father's House,* (NJ: P & R Publishing, 1996), p.6.
[68] Ibid., p. 42.
[69] Ibid., p. 43.
[70] A. W. Pink, p. 113-115.
[71] Much of the materials used in the appendixes are taken from Wayne Mack's *Homework Manual for Biblical Counseling.* (Phillipsburg: P & R Publishing, 1979).